WHEN ALL *HELL* BREAKS LOOSE...

facing your fiery trials with **FAITH**

by RICHARD ROBERTS

P.O. Box 2187
Tulsa, Oklahoma 74102

2496

Printed in the United States of America

TABLE OF CONTENTS

INTRODUCTION

What do you do when it seems like you're heading straight into the middle of a hellish situation? How can you keep from being swallowed up by the trials of life?

Trouble can come at a moment's notice in anyone's life. You're not immune to trouble, and neither am I. And when a difficult situation arises in your life, there are many things that can cause you to become tangled in the devil's snare. Intimidation may grip you, or Satan may try to attack you with guilt and condemnation.

The devil may hold your past up before you like a mirror and laughingly mock you with it. But you don't have to live with Satan's condemnation. The Bible says, *There is therefore now no condemnation to those who are in Christ Jesus* (Romans 8:1).

Something else that can hold you back is the old catchall, fear. Fear is one of the two master emotions of life—fear and faith. And the devil is the master of fear. But 2 Timothy 1:7 declares, *God has not given us a spirit of fear, but of power and of love and of a sound mind.* Through God, you can face the challenges of life with godly strength, love for yourself and others, healthy thinking, and a good attitude. The bad news doesn't have to get you down, and it certainly doesn't have to keep you down!

You may be in trying circumstances, but you can break free from the devil's snare. You can burst those bonds of intimidation. You can cast aside that fear and condemnation.

Isaiah 43:2 (NIV) proclaims, *When you pass through the waters, I will be with you; and when you pass through the rivers, they will not sweep over you. When you walk through the fire, you will not be burned; the flames will not set you ablaze.* I tell you, floods of problems may come… Winds of bad news may howl… The fires of danger may rage… But God has promised us that we will not be overcome if we'll stick with Him and use our faith until our victory comes.

Yes, you may have to walk through the roaring flames of the fire, but you don't have to stop in the middle of that mess! You can make a holy, determined decision that even if it seems like your world is falling apart, you will not be destroyed. I declare to you in the Name of Jesus, if you're down in the pit of despair right now, don't stay there. Look to God for rescue, and don't give in until you climb up out of that pit and find yourself standing on the mountaintops of blessing with the Lord!

Sounds easy, doesn't it? Well, it's not. However, it is altogether possible. And that's exactly what this book is all about—what to do when all hell breaks loose.

CHAPTER 1
OUT OF THE COMFORT ZONE

Have you heard the story of the boiling frog? It is said that if you place a frog in a pot of boiling water, it will try to escape. But if you put it in comfortable, cool water and turn the heat on very low, the frog will stay there, because it's comfortable. As the water slowly heats to a boil, the frog doesn't notice the temperature gradually increasing until it's too late. Soon, the frog will boil to death.

Maybe there's a situation in your life that isn't ideal. You're in a "pot" on the stove, so to speak, instead of in a nice pond. But you may have become so comfortable in your circumstances, even if they're unpleasant, that you've given up on trying to get out of them. Or maybe you want to get out of the bad circumstances you're in, but you've tried everything you know to do. You've done everything that worked in the past, but this time it doesn't seem to be helping. Maybe these circumstances have been something you've suffered so long in your life, you wouldn't know what it's like to live any other way.

I'm here to tell you that you don't have to stay in bad circumstances. It doesn't matter how comfortable your problem situation has become—if it's a problem, then you serve a God who has a solution for you. All things are possible with God, even that situation in your life that has seemed so impossible up to now. But to get free and move forward in a new way, you've got to be willing to do something about the situation you're in. You've got to break free from your comfort zone and launch out toward your miracle with a mighty leap of faith.

In Matthew 12:9–13, there's a dramatic scene where the Lord Jesus Christ called a man out of his comfort zone. The Bible says that Jesus was ministering in the synagogue one day when all of a sudden He looked up and saw a man who had a withered hand. I want you to read the story:

Now when He [Jesus] *had departed from there, He went into their synagogue. And behold, there was a man who had a withered hand. And they* [the religious leaders] *asked Him, saying, "Is it lawful to heal on the Sabbath?"* [And they asked this so] *that they might accuse Him.*

Then He said to them, "What man is there among you who has one sheep, and if it falls into a pit on the Sabbath, will not lay hold of it and lift it out? Of how much more value then is a man than a sheep? Therefore it is lawful to do good on the Sabbath." Then He said to the man, "Stretch out your [withered] hand." And he stretched it out, and it was restored as whole as the other.

Luke's Gospel is even more specific. It says that the man's *right hand* was withered (Luke 6:6).

Your right hand represents your strength. Most people in the world are right-handed, so when the Bible talks about your right hand, it's talking about your ability to handle the needs of life. When Jesus saw that this man had a withered right hand, He understood more about the man's emotional and spiritual condition as well.

I want you to know that the Lord Jesus Christ sees you this very moment in the situation you're in. He knows who you are. He knows where you live. He knows what you're going through. He sees your struggles, your turmoil, your heartache. And He can help you get out of the pit of trouble you've been living in.

In the same way that Jesus sees you, He also saw the man with the withered hand. He saw the man's need. The religious leaders were there too, but they weren't paying attention to the man or his needs. They were focused on their own needs instead. The religious leaders decided to ask Jesus a question, but their question was really a trick. They were trying to trap the Lord, to accuse

Him of a crime, so they posed a cunning question to Him that shows they cared more about making a religious point than about seeing a man healed. They asked Jesus, "Is it right to heal on the Sabbath day?"

You see, the Law of Moses said that the Jewish people were not to do any work on the Sabbath as a way to rest and to honor God, who also rested from His labor after creation (Genesis 2:2; Exodus 20:10). So, if Jesus had said, "Yes, it's okay to heal on the Sabbath," the religious leaders would have accused Him of blasphemy and violating God's Word.

But Jesus knew they were planning evil against Him, so He cut right through their smoke screen and replied, "Which one of you has a sheep? And should it fall into a pit on the sabbath, would you not go and rescue it from the pit?"

Oh, it's so easy for someone to fall into a pit! If that's where you are today, you can know that you're not alone. You're not the only person to end up in a troubling situation, and you're not the only one who has turned to God for rescue.

David was a man who found himself "in a pit," hiding in a cave to escape the javelin of King Saul (1 Samuel 24:3). But eventually he was delivered from Saul's persecution and was made king over Israel. And notice he never had to strike at Saul to be delivered.

Joseph also was cast into a pit, thrown there by his very own brothers (Genesis 37:24). He was sold into slavery, but eventually he was promoted to become the Pharaoh's right hand man. It didn't happen overnight. But it happened.

The prophet Jeremiah was locked up in a dungeon by evil men because he refused to stop prophesying the word of the Lord (Jeremiah 38:6). But he was eventually delivered out of the dungeon. And through it all, he never stopped prophesying.

Daniel was cast into a pit—a lions' den—all because he prayed to the Lord when he was told not to pray. But God sent His angel down into that den and padlocked the lions' jaws (Daniel 6:22).

God delivered each one of these people from their pit through His miraculous power. And I've got news for you today. You may have stumbled headlong into a bad situation—a situation that you don't know how to get out of—but I believe God has a good plan to bring you out.

Your Pit Can Become a Comfort Zone

Pits are terrible things. They are what I call "the nowhere zone." The nowhere zone is when you're halfway between where you were and where you want to be. A nowhere zone is another name for a comfort zone. And as long as you stay in your comfort zone, you are going nowhere.

Jesus Christ realized that the man with the withered hand had fallen into a pit of infirmity, and his handicap had become his comfort zone. The man was comfortable with his infirmity. He had grown accustomed to his withered hand.

What does it mean when we say something is withered? It means that it lacks moisture. It isn't supple or flexible. It has dried up. Many Christians today have a dryness or a lack of moisture in their lives. Sometimes we lack the moisture of the *rivers of living water* Jesus promises us in John 7:38.

When you have something that's withered in your life, you don't want to be out in front of the crowd. Oftentimes you're embarrassed by the problem, and you may try to hide it. You may force yourself to muster up a smile, because you don't want anybody to know that something is wrong.

Oh, the "withered hands" of life! A withered hand can represent anything that's troubling you. It can be a sin, a fault, or a shortcoming that continually tries to trip you up. It can be a devastating setback or a shameful secret from your past. It can be a crippling, death-dealing disease, a fear, a nagging doubt, or some other satanic attack of the devil. But I believe Jesus Christ is saying to you and me today, "It's time to stretch out that withered hand. It's time to make a move toward God!"

Perhaps this man was cowering in the back of the room, trying to vanish into the shadows, when Jesus called him out of the crowd, saying, *Rise up, and stand forth* (Luke 6:8 KJV). In other words, I believe He was telling the man, "Come out of the darkness. Come out of your comfort zone."

Then the Lord told him, "Stretch out your hand." Now, how on earth can you stretch out something which cannot be stretched out? I mean, the man's hand was limp and useless. In the natural, there was no way he could stretch it out. And yet Jesus commanded him to do it.

An incident stands out in my mind that clearly illustrates what I'm talking about here. Some years ago I was preaching in Calgary, Alberta, Canada, and a man who had suffered from agonizing back problems for twenty years came forward for prayer. Instead of laying my hands on him, I simply said, "My brother, bend over three times."

"I can't bend over," he blurted out. "That's why I came for prayer!"

That man resisted me because I asked him to step out of his comfort zone. So once again I repeated, "Please bend over three times." Well, he rolled his eyes at me as if he thought I was out of my mind.

Very reluctantly, he started to bend over. The first time he tried, he couldn't bend down very far, so he looked at me as if to say, "See, I told you so!"

"Bend over a second time," I insisted. The second time he could bend over a little farther, and the third time he could bend all the way down to the floor.

In utter amazement, he looked up at me and exclaimed, "What did you do?"

"I didn't do anything," I replied. It was the Lord who had healed him.

I believe God healed that man because he broke free from his comfort zone. And God wants us to abandon our safe little comfort zone and launch out in a great leap of faith toward Him!

I believe Jesus is saying to you today, "Stand forth! Stretch out your withered hand. Take a step toward your miracle." Yes, it may be difficult, and there may be people who will try to hinder you. There may be some who will tell you that God has lost His power, that He cannot restore what has become withered in your life. But you must make up your mind who you believe. Do you believe the Bible, or do you believe what the world says?

Jesus told the man to stretch out his hand, and as the man obeyed, the healing power of the Lord surged through his hand and he was made whole! It made the religious people mad, but it made Jesus glad. And I believe that if you will stretch out your faith, just as the man stretched out his hand, God will move in on the scene with a mighty outpouring of His power, which will enable you to begin to get out of your comfort zone and get into a position to receive the miracle you so desperately need.

The What-Ifs of Life

From Genesis to Revelation, the Bible is packed with the stories of men and women who had to step out of their comfort zones before they could receive a miracle. But I wonder what would have happened if they had balked at the will of God and refused to move out of their comfort zones?

For example, what would have happened if Noah had refused to budge from his comfort zone when God commanded him to build the ark? (See Genesis 6.) What if Noah had started resisting the Lord and arguing, "What's rain? And what's a boat?" You see, in Noah's day it had never rained before the Flood.

Or what if Noah had asked God, "What do You mean, build an ark? I don't think I can do that." Or, "Why do You want me to gather my family and a male and female of all the animals and load them onto the ark? That makes no sense."

What if Noah had decided to stop halfway through the construction of the ark? What if he had put his hands on his hips and said, "God, do You see how these people are mocking me? They're saying, 'Look at poor Noah! He's building a boat. What's a boat anyway? Noah, get that ark out of the street! It's an eyesore to the whole neighborhood!' I can't go on doing this. It's too embarrassing."

What if Noah had refused to step out of his comfort zone? I'll tell you the answer: Noah and his entire family would have been wiped out with the rest of humankind in the Flood. They would have been drowned with the ungodly, and God would have had to find another way to save a righteous remnant (Genesis 7–8).

Let me ask you another question. What if Moses had refused to step out of his comfort zone and take off his shoes when God said, "Moses, you're standing on holy ground" (Exodus 3:5)? What if he had refused to leave his old, familiar surroundings in the wilderness, where he had been wandering for forty years, a fugitive from Pharaoh?

Or what if Moses had gone to Egypt as God had commanded him and called down the great plagues upon Pharaoh, but then decided he didn't want to smear blood on the doorposts as the Lord had instructed him to do in Exodus 12?

What if Moses had declared, "Now listen, God, by Your power I've turned the river of Egypt into blood. I've called down frogs, lice, flies, boils, hailstones, and locusts. But I really don't want to kill a little lamb and smear its blood on the doorposts"?

I'll tell you what if. The death angel wouldn't have passed over Israel. Not only would the firstborn of Egypt have perished that night, but all the firstborn of Israel would have died too.

Or what if David, as a young shepherd, had refused to step out of his comfort zone? Can't you just picture him, clutching the sandwiches he had brought to his brothers who were on the front lines with King Saul? All of a sudden he sees Goliath strutting back and forth across the valley, casting a giant's shadow over the land (1 Samuel 17).

What if David had cut and run, yelling, "Just give me my sandwiches and I'll go on back home"? Or what if he had proposed, "Oh, yes, I'll fight the giant, but only if I can wear Saul's armor"?

I believe that if David had come out dressed in a suit of armor, Goliath wouldn't have had to lift his visor to laugh at the teenage boy who was running toward him, because David wouldn't have been running. He would have been crawling at a snail's pace, weighed down by armor that didn't fit him.

If Goliath hadn't raised his visor, he never would have exposed his forehead, which was the only vulnerable spot on his whole body. I believe if David had refused to come out of his comfort zone, that giant would have pulverized him.

And what if the four starving lepers who sat at the gates of Samaria—stranded between a fortressed city and the enemy army that surrounded it—had sighed to each other, "Let's sit here until we die"? (See 2 Kings 7.)

What if, at twilight, as they pondered whether or not they should launch out on a great march of faith and surrender themselves to the mercies of their enemies, one had announced, "Brothers, I believe it's too dark for us to strike out on such a dangerous mission. And besides, who are we to go out and face the enemy alone? Why, we're the least likely ones to do the job"?

I'll tell you what if. Those men would have starved to death at the gates of the city.

And what if Jesus Christ Himself had said no to God the Father and refused to step out of His comfort zone? I mean, He had a good thing going—a miracle ministry and an enthusiastic following. He had every reason to live.

What if Jesus had decided to call down a whole legion of angels to save Him instead of laying down His life? What if, in the Garden of Gethsemane, Jesus had cried out, "Father, I don't want to go to the Cross after all! I know it sounded like a good idea when I was up there in heaven, but now I'm not so sure about it. I don't want to have My hands and feet nailed to a tree, or a spear thrust into My side. This is as far as I'm going. I'm heading back to Nazareth to become a carpenter again"?

I'll tell you what if. If Jesus hadn't gone to the Cross, you and I wouldn't have had an opportunity to be saved from our sins. We wouldn't be washed in the blood of the Lamb. We wouldn't know Jesus Christ as our Lord and Savior.

A Way Out of the Comfort Zone

Now, all of us have comfort zones, and many times we do not like to come out of them. Why? Because it's easier to stay in the comfort zone. There are no risks there. There are no hurdles to overcome.

But comfort zones are also a terrible bondage. They're boxes, and it's difficult to break out of boxes because Satan can wrap them so tightly around you that you'll think there is no way out.

But, praise God, Jesus has made a way for us to get out of all the boxes the devil tries to trap us in. If we want to get out of the situation we're in, we have to break out of our comfort zones. If we step out by faith, I believe the Lord will launch us out to do great exploits for our God!

Believe You Can, and the How-To Will Show Up

Are there things God has called you to do, but you've been stuck in your comfort zone, wondering whether or not you'll ever be able to accomplish those things? If you'll believe God to help you and guide you forward, I believe the how-to will show up. Remember what Jesus said: *All things are possible to him who believes* (Mark 9:23). You see, God doesn't call the equipped. He equips the called.

When you believe that you can do what God has called you to do and be, and as you step out in faith, the how-to shows up. But if you don't step out, the how-to isn't going to show up.

I remember so well the story of a man in the Bible who had to step out of his comfort zone and believe that the how-to would show up. In Mark 9, Jesus and three of His disciples had descended from the Mount of Transfiguration to find that the other nine disciples were trying to minister to a man whose son was grievously tormented by a demon.

When the father first took the boy to the disciples, no doubt his heart was supercharged with faith. Certainly he must have heard about the remarkable miracles Jesus had performed. Perhaps he had heard about the way the Lord had cast a whole legion of demons out of the man from Gadara.

No doubt he must have thought, *If Jesus can cast out a legion of demons, surely He can take care of one demon that's plaguing my child.* Yet no matter how hard the disciples prayed, they couldn't break Satan's grip off his son.

There the man stood, in the presence of nine of the most trusted men upon the face of the earth, and they had failed miserably. Fear must have gripped his heart. At first he was filled with faith, but now his heart was flooded with doubt.

Then he saw Jesus Christ walking toward him, and he cried out, "Jesus, Your disciples couldn't deliver my son. But if You can do anything, please help us." As if the Lord of the universe couldn't do anything. Because of the disciples' inability to cast the demon out of the boy, the man's doubts had been magnified. He was saying, "God, if You can do anything," to the One who had created all things.

How many times have you and I gone to God in our humanness and exclaimed in exasperation, "Lord, I've done everything I know to do. If You can do anything about this situation, please help me," as if God wasn't capable of doing what needed to be done?

What was Jesus' response? First of all, He addressed the disciples, saying, in essence, "How long am I going to have to put up with your unbelief?" Then He turned to the boy's father and declared, *"If you can believe, all things are possible to him who believes"* (Mark 9:23).

Those are strong words, and I want you to take a moment to let them sink down into your spirit. Jesus was saying, "You can have *whatever* you can believe for." That is a powerful thought!

The man cried out and said with tears, "Lord, I do believe, but I still have this one little pocket of unbelief over here that I don't know how to deal with. Lord, please help me with my unbelief."

That's the way so many of us are today. Our hearts are filled with faith. Yet there is still a little twinge of doubt over in one corner of our minds, and it crops up to torment us every now and then. But Jesus Christ is telling us that we can take our faith, which is our launching pad for miracles, and believe with it, and the how-to will show up.

Next, the Lord commanded them, "Bring the boy to Me." Then He rebuked the foul spirit that was plaguing the child, and with a violent cry it wrenched his body as it left him. The boy collapsed in a heap on the ground, and the crowd gasped, thinking he must be dead. *But Jesus took him by the hand and lifted him up, and he arose* (Mark 9:27).

That young man was set free from the stranglehold of the devil, all because his father launched out in faith and the how-to showed up. And to receive your miracle, you, too, have to launch out and believe that you can and then expect the how-to for your miracle to show up in your life.

CHAPTER 2
JESUS: OUR EXAMPLE OF VICTORY IN HARD TIMES

Even the Lord Jesus, who is our example of how to live as an overcomer, had to get out of His comfort zone in order to move into God's best for His life. When Jesus stepped into the muddy waters of the Jordan River to be baptized by John the Baptist, He did it in obedience to God's Word. In the next instant, the heavens opened and the Holy Ghost appeared in the bodily form of a dove, fluttered down to earth, and landed upon the Lord. *Suddenly a voice came from heaven, saying, "This is my beloved Son, in whom I am well pleased"* (Matthew 3:17).

The prophecy of old was fulfilled when John dipped Jesus under the water of the Jordan. The Bible says, *Then Jesus, being filled with the Holy Spirit, returned from the Jordan and was led by the Spirit into the wilderness* (Luke 4:1). Now, that's a power-packed verse from the Bible!

Two things happened when Jesus obeyed God's Word through His baptism. First of all, the Bible says that He was full of the Holy Ghost, and second, that He was led by the Spirit into the wilderness. Mark's Gospel says that the Holy Spirit *drove* Him into the wilderness (Mark 1:12).

That is not a picture of God's Spirit gently nudging Jesus along the wilderness highway. The Living Bible says that Jesus was *urged by the Spirit out into the barren wastelands of Judea* (Luke 4:1). There was an urgency about the Spirit's promptings.

The Holy Spirit was driving the Lord Jesus Christ out into the barren wastelands of Judea, pressing Him to complete His mission for the Father. Most people shudder when they think about God's Spirit sending them into a barren wasteland, much less driving them toward their destination with great force.

But let's take this one step further. Another translation says that the Spirit of God led Jesus into the desert *in order to be tempted by the devil* (Matthew 4:1 Weymouth). Not only did the Spirit of God drive the Lord into a barren wasteland, but He drove Him there for the express purpose of being tempted by Satan. What on earth was going on here?

When Jesus was full of the Holy Ghost, the tempter came. It's important to recognize that when you're full of the Holy Spirit, when the anointing of God is upon you, that's when the tempter comes! If you're walking side by side with the devil, you'll never meet him face-to-face. It's only when you're doing something for God that you meet Satan head on.

How did the tempter come against Jesus? First of all, he came against His flesh. Jesus was led into a desert wilderness by the Holy Spirit, and for forty days and forty nights Satan badgered and harassed Him. During that time, the Bible says that Jesus fasted.

Now the only other person in the Bible who fasted for that length of time was the prophet Moses, so this is not a pattern that's being held up as a biblical example for us today. Of course, there may be special times when a person might feel led to fast a meal here and there, or occasionally fast for a day or two at a time. The apostle Paul said he fasted often (2 Corinthians 11:27). Short, regular fasts are the types of fasts that are held up as the model for New Testament believers.

But this moment for Jesus was unique. He was about to start His ministry, which would lead Him to the cross! Perhaps this is why He was led to do an unusually long fast in a wilderness location. And after this fast in the heat of the desert sun, He must have felt exhausted and famished. With that in mind, I want you to picture Jesus at the end of forty days in a desert wilderness, without food, trying to stand up, His body weak, His strength gone. And there was the tempter, the devil, staring Him in the face.

Notice that the devil came against Jesus when He was at His weakest physically. Don't think for a moment that Satan is going to come against you when you're operating at full force! He always comes when there is some kind of weakness he can latch onto. He is always searching for a victim to devour (1 Peter 5:8).

Jesus was weak with hunger when Satan came at Him, saying, "If You really are the Son of God, why don't You command these stones to be made into bread?" There must have been some stones nearby that looked like loaves of bread. A man who was exceedingly hungry could look with great longing at a pile of bread-shaped stones and be tempted to grab one and try to devour it. But Jesus wasn't moved by Satan's words. The only thing that moved the Lord was the voice of Father God.

Satan Came Against Jesus, and He'll Come Against You

Before we go any further, I want to draw your attention to the phrase the devil used when he tempted Jesus. He said, *"If You are the Son of God"* (Luke 4:3). Now, Satan already knew that Jesus Christ was the Son of God. Ezekiel 28:14 says that Lucifer, who later became the devil, was the covering angel, the one who covered the very person of the Almighty.

He was the most magnificent and brightest of all the archangels. He was present in the beginning when the morning stars sprang from the darkness. He knew Jesus Christ when Jesus, the Father, and the Holy Spirit created the world and made human beings.

Yet now, all of a sudden, Satan is acting as though he has had a memory lapse! He's saying, *"If You are the Son of God."* You see, the devil always comes to sow doubt in your mind about who Jesus is, what Jesus said, and what Jesus has done. And he even tried to sow doubt into Jesus' mind. That's how Satan operates—he is a liar and the father of lies (John 8:44).

Don't you dare believe him when he tells you that the Lord hasn't really healed you. Don't you dare believe him when he tells you that the seeds you've sown are just money cast into the wind. Don't you dare believe him when he tells you that you are serving God for nothing.

Satan taunted Jesus, "If You really are the Son of God, why don't You command these stones to be turned into piping-hot loaves of bread?" What a temptation for someone who hadn't eaten for forty days and forty nights.

The devil was coming at Jesus' flesh—at His weakest point. And I've got news for you. If Satan came against the flesh of Jesus and the weakness of Jesus, he will come against your flesh and your weakness too.

Satan will do everything in his power to try to get you over into the realm of the flesh. There are many people today who love God; yet they have fallen prey to the temptations of their flesh, and they have slipped and fallen into sin.

Look at the story of King David in 2 Samuel 11–12. Here was a man after God's own heart, and yet Satan caught him at the point of his weakness—his flesh—and he fell into sin. One day when David should have been out on the battlefield, marching against the enemies of Israel, for some reason he decided to stay behind at the palace. Oh, what a fateful decision!

The king was restless, pacing back and forth on the roof, when suddenly he noticed a lovely woman bathing nearby. Instead of showing respect for her privacy by turning away, he watched her and lusted after her. Then, in the heat of passion, he took things one step further and sent for her.

After they had spent the night together, Bathsheba became pregnant. David was so terrified that his evil deed would be discovered that he tried to trick Bathsheba's husband, Uriah, into coming back from the battlefield and sleeping with her himself, but Uriah refused. So David sent him into the thick of the battle where he knew the man would be killed.

After Uriah's death, the prophet Nathan confronted David with his sin. The great king of Israel repented before God, but he still paid a terrible price when Bathsheba's baby died (2 Samuel 12:13–19).

Yes, Satan will come against your flesh. He'll tell you, "It's all right to sleep with that person just this once." Or he'll tell you, "If you go ahead and steal that money, no one will ever know." He'll whisper in your ear, "If you'll just take these illegal drugs, you'll feel so much better." His temptations are being paraded everywhere you look. There's no shortage of the availability of sin.

So, how did Jesus overcome Satan's temptation against His flesh? He used God's Word as a weapon and said, *"It is written, 'Man shall not live by bread alone* [or man shall not live by his flesh], *but by every word of God'"* (Luke 4:4). He was quoting Deuteronomy 8:3 and saying, "We must live by what God says." I want you to notice that He didn't say we should live by half the words that God speaks, but by every word that comes out of the mouth of God.

Let me draw your attention to the fact that Jesus never spoke His own words to Satan. He never tried to match wits with the devil. He never tried to take Satan on in His humanity. He used that which is eternal—the Word of God, the sword of the Spirit. He said, "It is written," because the Word of God cuts through Satan's lies like a sharp knife.

When the devil launches an attack against me, I don't sit down and have a conversation with him. I don't try to reason with him. I don't try to analyze and figure out his strategy. I do what Jesus did. I quote the Word of God to him, because God's Word can put the devil's attack to a stop.

When Satan comes against your flesh, tell him, "It is written," and then begin to quote the Scriptures out loud to him. You're not only driving him away from your flesh by the Word, but also you're building up your faith, for *faith comes by hearing, and hearing by the word of God* (Romans 10:17). The most precious words you can ever hear or say are the words of God Almighty!

Satan Tempted Jesus with the Desires of His Heart

Since his first temptation didn't work, the devil tried again. He took Jesus up to the top of a high mountain and showed Him all the kingdoms of this world and their wealth and glory. Then he said, "I'll give You all this power and splendor if You'll just bow down and worship me" (Luke 4:5–7).

Just picture for a moment all the glory of this earth, all the glittering cities, the capitals of the nations, the reigning kings and leaders, the great masses of people, the gold and silver, the diamonds on the fingers of the wealthy ladies and gentlemen, the hidden treasures, the fine parades, all the wonders of the world displayed in a moment of time.

Now remember, Jesus' divine destiny was to rule over the kingdoms of this earth. He knew that was part of His ultimate mission. So the devil whispered slyly, "Jesus, You're at the threshold of the most anointed ministry the world has ever known. I have something to give You that's befitting Your great mission. You've wanted it ever since You were a little boy, and all You have to do to get it is bow down to me."

Satan came against Jesus through His desires, and he comes against you and me in exactly the same way. The devil will try to pervert your God-given desires. He'll lay out before you everything you can have if you will bow down and worship him.

You may be thinking, *Doesn't the Bible say that God will give me the desires of my heart?* Of course it does, but it does not say that He will give you the desires of your mind. Yes, Satan will show you what you can have if you will only allow your mind to rule over your spirit. But God created us to keep our minds in subjection to our spirits. That's what 2 Corinthians 10:5 means when it says that we are to *cast down arguments and every high thing that exalts itself against the knowledge of God, bringing every thought into captivity to the obedience of Christ.*

How did Jesus handle this temptation? He told Satan, "*For it is written, 'You shall worship the Lord your God, and Him only you shall serve'*" (Luke 4:8). He was saying, "Devil, I'm going to get My desires met in the right way!"

The Son of God said, "Devil, it is written," and He repulsed Satan and defeated him by using God's Word. And you and I can do the same thing with our faith in His Word.

Satan Tempted Jesus with Pride

Before Jesus was tempted in the wilderness, He had just had a tremendous peak experience with His heavenly Father. The God of all creation had sent a powerful sign to confirm Jesus' ministry. After being baptized in the Jordan River, the Lord waded out of the water, the heavens opened, the Spirit of the Lord descended upon Jesus in the bodily form of a dove, and an audible voice thundered from above, saying, "*This is My beloved Son, in whom I am well pleased*" (Matthew 3:17).

Talk about success! The Most High God had given Jesus Christ His own personal endorsement. What if God the Father told everybody how great you were? What if He sent the Holy Spirit to light upon your head like a gentle, fluttering dove? What if He told the whole world that you were His beloved Son and He was well pleased with you? You'd probably be tempted to be full of yourself, wouldn't you?

Pay close attention to what I'm about to say next. After you've experienced an outstanding success, don't be surprised to see the devil arriving to tempt you. He'll try to sell you on yourself. He'll tell you that you don't need God's help anymore. Really, I believe you have to guard yourself even more when you've had a big success than you do when you've experienced a shattering setback.

The devil comes and tells you, "Look what you did! No one can defeat you now!" Watch out when that happens. Proverbs 16:18 says that pride can lead to destruction. And Proverbs 13:10 tells us, *By pride comes nothing but strife.* Pride is something the devil tries to use against us, and all it causes is trouble.

There's something else I want to point out to you about the devil's tactics here. When he heard Jesus say, "It is written," he thought to himself, *Now that's a good line. I ought to use that line myself!* So with his next temptation, Satan began to mimic the Lord.

Jesus had quoted Scriptures to the devil, so Satan turned around and quoted Scriptures back to Him. He took Jesus to the pinnacle of the temple in Jerusalem and said, *If thou be the Son of God, cast thyself down from hence: For it is written, He shall give his angels charge over thee, to keep thee: And in their hands they shall bear thee up, lest* ***at any time*** *thou dash thy foot against a stone* (Luke 4:9–11 KJV).

I want you to turn in your Bible to Psalm 91:11–12 and read the passage Satan was referring to here. Notice that in the King James Version of Luke 4:11, Satan tucked in three extra words—*at any time*—which were not in the original text.

This Scripture in the Psalms actually says, *For he shall give his angels charge over thee, to keep thee in all thy ways. They shall bear thee up in their hands, lest thou dash thy foot against a stone.* It does not say "lest **at any time** you dash your foot against a stone." In other words, God isn't saying that you can jump off the top of a building at any time you feel like it, and He will send His angels to catch you in their arms. That kind of reckless behavior would be tempting the Lord, and that's not what this Scripture is talking about.

We can never falsify a Scripture, take it out of context, or misapply it and think that it will work. It will not! God is not obligated to perform His Word when it has been misapplied, falsified, or perverted.

Satan mimicked Jesus by quoting Scriptures back to Him, but he misquoted the Word of God. Jesus cut through the devil's lie when He replied, *"The Scriptures also say, 'You must not test the Lord your God'"* (Luke 4:12 NLT). That's a reference to Deuteronomy 6:16, and it shows that Jesus knew not just part of the Word—He knew all of it. He used the Word of God in context, and that kept Him on the right path when Satan tried to deceive Him.

It's so important to realize how Satan loves to take a portion of the Word of God, quote it to you, and make it sound right. And he loves to appeal to your pride as a way to get you off track.

What does pride do in your life? First of all, it causes you to make wrong decisions. It causes you to say things you will later regret. Satan said to Jesus, "Throw Yourself down from the top of the temple. God will protect You." You see, your pride says, "This sin won't really destroy me. I can get away with it just this once. I can take it right up to the edge, and it will be all right."

There are many Christians today who are living right on the edge, and they don't realize that they're about to slip over the edge because of their pride. You see, your pride can cost you everything.

I remember my father telling the story of a beautiful woman with flaming red hair who came in the prayer line at one of his crusades. She was an opera singer who had lost her voice, and it had cut off her ability to earn her living as a singer.

Many people knew who this woman was. When she came into the prayer line, the Holy Spirit revealed to my dad that she was dealing with a pride issue. My father said to her, "Ma'am, I want you to run up and down the center aisle seven times as a point of contact for God to heal your voice." (That's a lot like what the prophet Elisha said when he told the Syrian general, Naaman, to dip in the Jordan River seven times and he'd be healed of leprosy in 2 Kings 5.)

Immediately she bristled, stuck her nose up in the air, turned around, and walked off. My dad just shrugged his shoulders and kept praying for the rest of the people in the prayer line.

A few minutes later, he looked up and saw this woman running down the center aisle toward him, her hands in the air, and tears streaming down her face. Then she turned around and ran back again. Seven times she repeated the process, and afterward she let out a joyous shout. God completely healed her! Why? Because she laid her pride at the feet of Jesus.

How Did Jesus Handle the Pride Issue?

When Satan said, "If You are the Son of God, throw Yourself down from the pinnacle of the temple, and the angels of God will catch You in their arms," Jesus answered him once again with the Word of God. He quoted Deuteronomy 6:16, saying, "Devil, it's also said, don't test the Lord." He was saying, "You shall not be a prideful person." It's so important for you to eliminate pride, or it will destroy you.

The Lord Jesus Christ dealt with the pride issue by aligning Himself with what the Word of God said. Notice that He began His encounter with the devil by quoting the Scriptures, He continued by quoting the Scriptures, and He ended His dealings with Satan by quoting God's Word.

The devil didn't start out with the Scriptures, but after he heard Jesus quote the Word of God a few times, he finally caught on. Then he began to quote some Scriptures too, but it didn't work for him because he twisted God's Word. Jesus knew better, and he refused to believe Satan's lies.

What does the Bible say happened to Jesus after He continued to quote the Word of God to the devil? It says, *Then the devil left him, and behold, angels came and ministered to him* (Matthew 4:11).

No one is exempt from Satan's attack. He's going to come against your flesh, your pride, and your desires in the same way that he came against the Lord Jesus. But if you will do what Jesus did, you can overcome the devil too. As a child of God, you are an overcomer made in the image of God. No matter what situation is happening in your life today, the Word of God can work for you, just as it worked for Jesus.

So, the next time Satan tries to get his hooks into you, just tell him, "Satan, it is written that I'm a blood-bought child of God. You may have come against me, but I don't have to let you win. Take that, devil, in Jesus' Name!"

CHAPTER 3
STEP INTO THE RIVER

As our example, Jesus shows us that when you find yourself in the middle of a bad situation, it's absolutely vital for you to keep your attitude right. Why? Because in hard times, it's so easy to get discouraged, to fixate on the problem instead of on God's Word, or to focus on our past mistakes instead of our hope for the future. Sometimes, that requires us to call on the Holy Spirit for divine help in making an attitude adjustment, letting go of past failures, rekindling our hope, and standing in faith.

In John 7:37–39, the Lord gives us the Bible formula for opening up our lives to the Holy Spirit. This scene takes place on the last great day of the Jewish Feast of Tabernacles, when Jesus did something that had never been done before, and He did it in a rare, emphatic way. Jesus broke all tradition when He stopped the processional and shouted:

"If anyone thirsts, let him come to Me and drink. He who believes in Me, as the Scripture has said, out of his heart will flow rivers of living water." But this He spoke concerning the Spirit, whom those believing in Him would receive; for the Holy Spirit was not yet given, because Jesus was not yet glorified.

Jesus was saying, "If anyone is grappling with a problem, if anyone thirsts to get from where he is to where he wants to be, let him come to Me!"

You know, God makes the answer so clear! It's so simple that it's profound.

Now, this dramatic event took place before the outpouring of the Holy Spirit. Thank God, we're living in the day when the Spirit of God has already been poured out, and His Spirit does not need to be poured out a second time. He is here where I am, and He's there where you are. He's ready to flood your whole being with the wonder-working power of God!

You see, if we want to make it through the trials and troubles of life, we've got to plunge into the river of God's Spirit. If we want to leave the past behind and make a fresh, new start in our lives, we have to learn how to open up the tap so the Spirit of God can flow through our lives.

Let Go of Your Past Failures

Leaving your comfort zone behind and moving toward your miracle sometimes requires you to let go of past failures, mistakes, and fears. Back in the days of the Old West, when tragedy struck people's lives, they would simply jump on their horse or buy a ticket on the nearest stagecoach and relocate in some other town where no one would recognize them. They could remain anonymous or hide their past. In the Old West, it was common to hear someone say that a cowboy was "riding with a secret." That meant there was something in his past that he wanted to overcome, so he was looking for a new place to start afresh.

A lot of people today are walking around with a secret. You may have a secret of your own. Nobody else knows about it. But you and God know about it, and you're wondering if life is ever going to be any different. I tell you, it's only going to be different if you allow the Holy Spirit to help you let go of the past and move into the bright future that God has for you.

You don't have to handle your past like they did in the Old West. If you want to start your life anew, today is the time and where you are right now is the place. You can turn to God, and He can help you start over, right where you are. No matter what has happened to you, no matter what mistakes you may have made, the time to put the past in the past is now. And you can call upon the Holy Spirit to help you do that.

The apostle Paul declared, "There's not one single thing I can do about the past. All I can do is give it to the Lord. Then I can lift my head up and press on toward the mark for the prize of the high calling of God in Christ Jesus" (see Philippians 3:13–14).

There is a prize out there, and it's worth attaining. But in order to lay hold of the prize, we're going to have to let go of the past, move forward, and keep our attitudes right.

The Holy Spirit Can Help You Make the Right Choice

Is God's spiritual river flowing in your life today? Are you being refreshed in the Spirit, or are you feeling spiritually stale? Are you free in the Spirit, or are you hindering the flow of God's Spirit? Are you overflowing, or are you stagnant?

Let me illustrate in geographical terms what I'm talking about here. In the nation of Israel, the Sea of Galilee is a magnificent body of water, a huge inland sea that's teeming with life. Why? Because water flows freely into it and also flows out of it.

If you follow its main inlet and outlet, the Jordan River, to the place where it empties into the Dead Sea, you'll notice that the water pours in, but nothing pours out. That's why it's called a "dead" sea. It's stagnant and lacking in life. In the same way, some of us Christians have become dry in our spirits.

Now, I want to ask you another question. Is anything jamming up the flow of God's Spirit in your life—things like unconfessed sin, pride, anger toward God or toward other people, unforgiveness, bitterness, depression, or just a general feeling of being down on yourself?

You may be thinking, *I can't seem to get over this problem, this attitude.* No, you can't do it by yourself. You need the active, energizing power of the Holy Spirit to help you.

Jesus declared, "Are any of you thirsty? Are any of you dry, and you feel like you're about to fall apart? Are you hurting? Alone? Troubled? Is there any sickness, heartache, loneliness? Are there money problems? Family problems? Relationship problems?" Then He added, "Come to Me and drink. Step into the river of God's life!"

I talk so much about the baptism of the Holy Spirit because He is the only One who can empower you to overcome your problems. I pray in tongues—the prayer language of the Spirit—every day of my life because I need His help. Like all people, I'm hit with decisions each day, and many times I don't have a clue as to what I should do. Aren't there times when you wish someone would tell you which path to take—to say, "Go this way," "Do this," or, "Do that"?

Maybe there's a decision hanging out there in front of you, and your heart is tugging you in one direction, while your mind is pulling you in another direction. That's when the Holy Spirit can help you make the right choice.

Tap into the Holy Spirit's Prayer

Perhaps you were raised in a denomination that teaches against the baptism of the Holy Spirit. You may not be accustomed to praying in the Holy Spirit, or you might not know much about it. However, every born-again believer has a Bible right to tap into the Holy Spirit's prayer. We can pray in our daily devotional prayer language any time we desire.

You may believe that speaking in tongues isn't for everybody, but in 1 Corinthians 14:5 (NIV), the apostle Paul said, *I would like every one of you to speak in tongues.* The baptism of the Holy Spirit is for every born-again believer.

It's Easy to Receive The Prayer Language of the Spirit

If you're a Christian, God's Spirit took up residence in your heart the day that you were born again. He bears witness with your spirit that you are a child of God (Romans 8:16).

Romans 8:26–27 clearly states that the Holy Spirit is interceding for us. He's praying seven days a week, twenty-four hours a day, in our behalf. All you have to do to connect with His prayers for you is to open up your heart and tap into the Spirit's prayer.

Some people have the mistaken idea that the Holy Spirit will somehow take control of their tongues and force them to speak, but nothing could be further from the truth. We have to decide to pray in tongues by an act of our human will. The apostle Paul said, "*I will* [I determine] *to pray with the Spirit, and I will also pray with the understanding* [in my own language]" (1 Corinthians 14:15).

That means you can pray in the Spirit anytime you want to. Anytime you're awake in the nighttime, anytime you're awake in the daytime, anytime you're happy, anytime you're sad, anytime there's trouble in your life, anytime there is a victory, you can pray in tongues.

Praying in the Spirit isn't some strange, mystical experience designed for a few fanatics somewhere on the fringe. It's one of the central Bible doctrines God has given to the church.

And it's not something that's hard to grasp. It's simply you and me talking to our heavenly Father in a language that only He understands. It's you and me praying out the mysteries of God, praying out His plans and purposes in our lives (1 Corinthians 14:2).

Praying in the Spirit builds you up as a Christian. Jude 20 NIV declares, *But you, dear friends, build yourselves up in your most holy faith and pray in the Holy Spirit.* With such a powerful, Biblical way to build up your faith, doesn't it make sense to consider making praying in the Spirit a priority in your life?

Step into the River

You may be afraid to speak in tongues. I remember one outstanding gospel singer who declined to appear as a guest on my television program. When I asked why, this person replied, "Richard, you speak in tongues, and I'm afraid the Holy Spirit will say something to me and scare me to death, and my ministry will be wrecked."

It's unfortunate that many Christians have been taught this way. Much of the church world today treats the Holy Spirit as if He is not even there. And yet He's the One who will lead you and guide you on a daily basis if you'll only let Him.

Without the baptism of the Holy Spirit, without God revealing His strategy to me by His Spirit, I don't think I could withstand the devil's onslaught. And I'm not the only one who has to withstand an onslaught. You do, too, because Satan wants to wreak havoc on God's plan for your life.

I tell you, it's time to get into the flow of the mighty Holy Spirit. The water isn't cold; it's just the right temperature. And it's fresh. It's clear. It's not shallow either. It's deep. It's a river flowing freely from the throne of God!

Jesus declared in John 7:37–38, "If any man is thirsty, if any woman is thirsty, if anyone is craving a change in his life, let him come to Me, and let him drink. Out of him will flow rivers of life!" I believe it's time for every born-again child of God to be filled with the Spirit and pray in tongues. It's time to put aside everything that has hindered you, open your life and heart to God, and step into the river of God's mighty Holy Spirit power.

If you would like for one of our Holy Spirit-anointed prayer partners to pray with you to begin praying in the Holy Spirit, I encourage you to call the Abundant Life Prayer Group at (918) 495-7777. They will pray for you personally.

CHAPTER 4
YOUR OBEDIENCE PRODUCES MIRACLES

One of the most unusual miracles of Elisha's entire ministry is found in 2 Kings 4:1–7. One day the wife of one of Elisha's fellow prophets went to him with some dreadful news. She told him, "My husband has died, and now his creditor says that he is coming to take my two sons and make them his slaves. Elisha, my sons are all I have left!"

There are people today who cringe every time the telephone rings because they're afraid it's another creditor threatening to take away their car, their home, their possessions, everything they hold dear. Perhaps some tragedy has struck their lives. Their spouse may have died, or they've lost their job and cannot pay their bills. They're frightened and are crying out to the Lord because they simply do not know what to do.

Willing Obedience Brings You God's Blessings

I want you to notice that when Elisha heard the widow's tragic story, his first response was, "What shall I do for you?" or, "What can I do about it?" And isn't that often our reaction when someone tells us about a terrible financial tragedy? We would love to be able to pay off the person's debts, but more often than not we can't.

Undoubtedly Elisha wasn't in a position to pay this woman's bills, but really, he was thinking about her problem in the natural. Sometimes I think we miss the whole point when we start thinking about people's problems in the natural.

We may not be able to pay off another person's debt, but we can pray for them. We can speak a word of encouragement to lift their spirits. We can give them the Word of God. And perhaps we can give them a word of deliverance from the throne room of heaven!

At first Elisha got over into the natural realm and asked, "How can I help you?" But then the power of God began to move upon him. All of a sudden, he began to view the widow's situation in a supernatural way. And when you move into the supernatural realm, you're moving into the realm of miracles. You're stepping into a holy flow of God's presence. And when you enter that realm, you can expect God to give you fresh revelation and a way to escape the devil's attack.

When Elisha began to tune in to the Spirit of God, the Lord prompted him to ask this widow an odd question. "What do you have in your house that you can sell?" he asked.

No doubt she must have scratched her head and thought about it for a moment. Then she replied, "The only thing I have is a little jug of oil." Praise God, a light bulb must have flashed on in Elisha's spirit when she spoke those words.

As soon as Elisha realized that her deliverance depended upon God's multiplying her jug of oil, he began to get excited. He knew the only thing that could limit her miracle was the degree to which she pressed in to the Lord with her faith. So he told her, "Borrow as many pots and pans from your friends and neighbors as you possibly can."

Now, I want you to think about this part of the miracle for a moment. What if she had gone to her friends and neighbors and halfheartedly gathered up only a meager supply of pots and pans? She wouldn't have received her miracle. Her miracle depended upon her full obedience to Elisha's instructions.

The widow couldn't have expected to receive her full deliverance with only a few pots and pans. It wouldn't have worked, because the oil could be multiplied only as long as there were pots and pans to be filled. And the more oil she ended up with, the more money she could raise to pay off her debts.

What am I driving at here? There's a reason that God asks for our complete obedience, not our partial obedience, not our halfway obedience, nor our halfhearted obedience. Isaiah 1:19 declares, *If you are willing and obedient, you shall eat the good of the land.*

Being willing speaks of an attitude of the heart. Mere outward obedience to God's Word won't produce much of a breakthrough in your life. But when you have a willing heart, a willing spirit, *and* you're obedient, the sky is the limit.

Close the Door on Distractions

Apparently this widow gathered up huge armloads of pots and pans—as many as she could find—and then she and her sons carefully followed the rest of Elisha's instructions. He told her, "Go into your house with your sons and shut the door behind you. Then pour the oil into the pots and pans, and set them aside as they are filled."

Why do you suppose Elisha told them to go into their house and shut the door behind them? Normally, most people would shut the door anyway, wouldn't they? I believe he didn't want to take any chances, so he spelled out his instructions step by step.

This woman and her sons were desperate. They had problems coming at them from every direction. First, her husband (their father) had died, and then his creditor was threatening to tear the rest of the family apart. It must have been an incredibly stressful time, and additional distractions would only have made things worse.

There are times in your life and mine when we have to close the door on everything that would deter us from receiving our miracle. We have to shut the door on the detractors, the critics, and the skeptics. We have to close out all the distractions of this life, the cares of this world, and the hectic nature of our daily affairs. When you need a miracle, you must learn how to shut the door on anything that would keep you from pressing in to God until you get your answer.

When the widow shut the door and she and her sons got alone with the Lord, something powerful happened in the spirit realm. Her little jug of oil began to bubble and hum with the life of God. Miracle-working power began to flow in her house.

She called to her sons, told them to start passing her the pots and pans, and then she began to pour. As she poured, the oil sloshed to the top of those pots and pans, and as soon as each one was full, she set it aside.

The whole room must have been jammed with pots and pans and jars, all filled to the brim with olive oil. Her sons had probably lined them up across the tabletops and countertops and even piled them all over the floor. What a sight it must have been! A few hours earlier as she sat in her little house, not knowing what to do or which way to turn, this widow never dreamed that such a miracle was possible. But now her miracle was happening right before her very eyes.

"Bring me another pan!" she exclaimed to her sons, who were just as flabbergasted as she was by the astonishing miracle God was performing for them.

"There aren't any more," they cried, and the Bible says that the oil stopped flowing. The widow went back to Elisha and told him what had happened, and then he gave her the rest of the miracle. He said, "Go, sell the oil, and pay your debts; and there will be enough money left over for you and your sons to live on."

Thank God, the Lord doesn't shut off His miracle power just as soon as our bare, essential needs are met. No—He gives us an extra, running-over portion (Luke 6:38). He takes care of our needs, but then He also gives us that extra supply to put us over the top. That's what I mean when I say, "God is not enough. He's *more* than enough!"

The apostle Paul put it this way: *Now glory be to God who by his mighty power at work within us is able to do far more than we would ever dare to ask or even dream of—infinitely beyond our highest prayers, desires, thoughts, or hopes* (Ephesians 3:20 TLB).

So, if you are in financial trouble or facing challenges on the job or lacking in something you need, don't give up hope. Do what this widow did. Just pour out what you have to the Lord, then watch our "too much" God pour out His abundant overflow into your life!

CHAPTER 5
WHATEVER YOU DO—DON'T COMPROMISE

When Satan tries to drag you into a bad situation or push you into a pit full of problems, just remember that you don't have to surrender to despair or doubt or fear. It's important to stand firm in your faith that God delivers us out of trouble (Psalm 34:17), because the world is filled with trouble.

Bad news is everywhere. But you don't have to let it get you down and crush you into hopelessness. If you're a Christian, you may live in this world but you are not of it (John 17:14–15). You don't have to do things the devil's way.

So, when the devil tries to stir up trouble in your circumstances, it's important to realize that you have power, through God, to resist the devil. Why? Because no one is immune to the ungodly forces that are erupting all across this earth. The devil comes against all Christians, because he wants to hinder us from doing God's will on the earth. The trials of life are going to come at you, no matter who you are or where you live.

You may say, "But, Richard, you're in the ministry. Surely the devil doesn't come at you the way he comes at me." Let me tell you, the devil knows my address as well as he knows yours! He hurls his fiery darts at me the same way he hurls them at you. My family and I are not immune to Satan's attacks.

I remember when our daughter Olivia, who was eight years old at the time, was struck by a violent illness. The vomiting and diarrhea persisted for two days until she became dangerously dehydrated. At four o'clock in the morning, we wound up in the emergency room at a local hospital. Somehow, through something she had eaten, she had contracted an infection of the deadly E. coli bacteria. Lindsay and I had heard about E. coli on the news but never imagined that one of our children might get it.

As Olivia lay in that hospital bed, quarantined, her tiny body almost lifeless, we took authority over that situation in the name of Jesus. We laid our hands on her and saturated her with our faith. We rebuked the devil's power. We prayed for two days, calling upon God, and commanding that sickness to leave her body! Our family and friends were praying with us too, and the doctor treating her was a Spirit-filled Christian, which helped us as we stood in faith for Olivia's healing.

Finally, after two and a half days, the symptoms stopped. Hearing our little girl's voice grow stronger made our hearts burst with joy.

People have said things to me like, "Richard, you're a healing evangelist. I didn't think things like that happened to you. I didn't think you faced the kinds of problems I face." Believe me, things like that do happen to me. I am one of Satan's targets, just like you are. He comes against all of God's children. But we don't have to let him win.

Every time I face troubles or trials, I remind myself that the devil may be trying to get to me, but I don't have to give in to him!

You have to take your stand against the forces of the devil coming against your life too. And by the grace of God, you can rise above your negative circumstances and overcome them by the power of God working in and through you.

If You Don't Bow, You Won't Burn

Imagine what Shadrach, Meshach, and Abednego must have experienced when they faced Nebuchadnezzar's burning fiery furnace, which the king heated seven times hotter than ordinary for their punishment (Daniel 3).

As you may recall, Shadrach, Meshach, and Abednego were among the young Hebrew men and women who were carried away as captives to Babylon by King Nebuchadnezzar's legions. I want you to picture them as they walked along the banks of the great Euphrates River, wondering how they could sing the songs of Zion in that distant land.

All of a sudden the air was filled with the sound of trumpets, flutes, cornets, and a variety of other musical instruments. Much to their astonishment, every Babylonian bowed on their faces and began to chant, "Great is Nebuchadnezzar our god! Great is Nebuchadnezzar our god!"

No doubt one of the Hebrews must have turned to a passing stranger and asked, "What does this mean?"

Then someone must have told them, "Haven't you heard? The king has set up a golden statue of himself, and when the music plays, everyone in the land must bow down on the ground and worship the image. Anyone who refuses to bow will be burned to death in a fiery furnace."

When Shadrach, Meshach, and Abednego heard Nebuchadnezzar's decree, the blood in their veins must have turned cold, but they still refused to bow, because they were willing to worship only the true God, Jehovah.

It didn't take long for the news of their disobedience to reach King Nebuchadnezzar. He called for the three Hebrews and gave them a second chance to bow. Believe me, Satan will always give you a second chance to bow. He'll give you every opportunity to give in to him.

The king declared, "If you bow to my golden image before all of my princes, my governors, my magicians, my family, and my staff, it will go well with you. But if you refuse, I'll cast you alive into a burning, fiery furnace! And who is the God that can deliver you out of my hands?"

Shadrach, Meshach, and Abednego looked straight into Nebuchadnezzar's eyes and saw his rage. They could feel the heat of his furnace as it was heated seven times hotter than ordinary.

But Shadrach, Meshach, and Abednego didn't budge an inch. They exclaimed, *"O Nebuchadnezzar, we have no need to answer you in this matter. If that is the case, our God whom we serve is able to deliver us from the burning fiery furnace, and He will deliver us from your hand, O king. But if not, let it be known to you, O king, that we do not serve your gods, nor will we worship the gold image which you have set up"* (Daniel 3:16–18).

And that brings me to one of the two inescapable laws in this life—the law of faith. The law of faith declares that if you don't bow, you won't burn. But there is another law, and it's the law of compromise. That law says that if you do bow, you will burn.

If you serve the Lord, your faith will be tried. If you love God, those who hate God will hate you. If you serve Him with all of your spirit, mind, and strength, then the devil's fury will be unleashed against you, and he'll try to trip you up so that you stop serving God. That's why you have to remember that even though trouble may rear its ugly head, you don't have to surrender your faith in God or your confidence that He will deliver you.

Now, I want you to pay close attention to what I'm about to say next. There will always be a Nebuchadnezzar. There will always be a fiery furnace. And there will always be an opportunity to compromise. But when you compromise, you generally lose what you sought to gain by compromising. In other words, if you compromise, you will pay the price.

You Can Survive the Fiery Furnace

Shadrach, Meshach, and Abednego proclaimed, "O king, we may burn in your furnace, but we will not bow to your golden image." Despite the threat they were under, they refused to let go of their faith in God.

Nebuchadnezzar flew into a rage as he shouted, "Stoke that furnace seven times hotter than ordinary, and throw those three men into the fire!" Then he called on his mightiest men, and as soon as they threw those young men into the fiery furnace, Nebuchadnezzar's men were consumed by the flames because they weren't made out of the right kind of stuff.

When the door to the furnace was slammed shut, Nebuchadnezzar must have thought, "That's it. It's settled. No one will ever dare to take me on again. The next time the music sounds, everybody will bow down and sing my song: 'Great is Nebuchadnezzar our god!'"

The king waited a while and then said to himself, "Those ropes ought to be burned up by now, and their clothing is bound to be engulfed in flames. Pretty soon we'll be able to smell their burning flesh."

So the three Hebrew men burned in the fire—or so everybody thought. A few minutes later, Nebuchadnezzar declared, "Open the door!" What he saw must have made his hair stand on end.

When Nebuchadnezzar peered into the fire, he saw the three young Hebrew men walking around unharmed in the middle of the flames. The king gasped when he looked in again, for he saw a fourth Man in the midst of the fire, and the fourth Man looked like the Son of God (Daniel 3:25).

At the very instant Nebuchadnezzar had Shadrach, Meshach, and Abednego thrown into the flames, Jesus Christ—the Fourth Man—met them in the midst of the fire. Before the flames could begin to burn them, God preserved their lives and surrounded them with His divine protection. So they started doing a victory march in the middle of the flames and praising God.

When Nebuchadnezzar called the three young men out of the furnace, he sniffed their clothing, but there was no smell of smoke upon them. Even their hair and skin were not singed. The king proclaimed, *If any people, whatever their race or nation or language, speak a word against the God of Shadrach, Meshach, and Abednego, they will be torn limb from limb, and their houses will be turned into heaps of rubble. There is no other god who can rescue like this* (Daniel 3:28–29 NLT).

When Shadrach, Meshach, and Abednego refused to compromise and bow to Nebuchadnezzar's golden image, they were thrown into a hellish situation. But they did not burn. They escaped from the fiery furnace unharmed.

Stand for God, and He Will Stand for You

Even though the devil has tried to defeat me time and time again, I've refused to surrender to him. I've made a decision that I'm going to resist the devil and stand for what God stands for. I've decided to honor the Lord, no matter what the cost.

You may be facing a battle of your faith today. Trouble, despair, discouragement, confusion, defeat—all of these things may be trying to take you over. But you don't have to surrender. You can make a faith-filled decision that the gates of hell are not going to prevail against you (Matthew 16:18). And when you take a stand for the Lord, you can expect Him to take a stand for you.

CHAPTER 6
WHEN YOU FALL, GET UP AGAIN

Sometimes, the trouble we find ourselves in is partly our own fault. The best example in the Bible of someone getting himself into a pit of trouble is Samson, the man of unmatched strength. The birth of Samson was supernatural. His mother had been barren all of her married life; then one day she was visited by an angel who had a message for her from the Lord. He revealed to her that she was going to have a son, and he also gave her divine instructions concerning the child. (See Judges 13.)

First of all, the angel commanded her not to drink wine or strong drink while she was carrying the baby or to eat anything that was contrary to the Jewish dietary laws. He also instructed her not to cut her son's hair, for he was to be a Nazarite from his birth—one separated unto God. Then he explained that the child was destined to deliver Israel from the Philistines.

You see, at that particular time, the people of God were being dominated by ungodly and cruel men—the Philistine nation—because of their disobedience to the Lord. Of course, nobody likes to be shoved around by his enemies. No doubt the children of Israel had been crying out to God for a deliverer, and He answered their cry by sending Samson.

Even as a young man, when the Spirit of the Lord came upon Samson, he could perform great feats of strength. But he also had a terrible weakness, and Satan used his weakness to enslave him and make him the laughingstock of the entire nation of Philistia.

In Judges 14, you'll notice that Samson was troubled by lust for heathen women. One day he strolled into the Philistine camp where he spotted a beautiful young woman, and he was so strongly attracted to her that he told his father and mother, "Get her for me. I want to marry her."

Samson's father was shocked by his request, because he was a devout Jewish man, and he wanted his son to marry a young Jewish woman. Besides, he knew that the hand of the Lord was upon Samson, and if he married someone of his own faith, it would be much easier for him to pursue his calling.

Strangely enough, the Bible says in verse 4 that the Lord was behind Samson's request to marry this Philistine girl because He was setting a trap to stir up a fight between Samson and the Philistines, who at that time ruled Israel. Isn't it amazing how God can use even our weaknesses to get us into a position to do what He's called us to do!

While Samson and his parents were on their way to make arrangements for Samson's marriage, the Bible says that a young lion roared against him from the forest. Like a bolt of lightning, the Spirit of the Lord came upon Samson, and he tore the lion to pieces with his bare hands. Then he and his parents continued on their way to meet his young bride's family.

As soon as Samson talked with the girl, his heart leaped with joy. He felt that she was surely the wife for him. Preparations were made for the marriage, and Samson and his parents returned home.

Later, when they were on their way back for the wedding, Samson decided to stop and look at the carcass of the lion. He was startled to discover that a swarm of bees had built a hive in its decaying body. So he scooped up some of the honey and took it to his parents, but he didn't tell anyone where it came from.

At the wedding feast, it was customary for several of the young men to accompany the groom. So the Philistines gave Samson a bachelor's party. For the next seven days, he and thirty young men were constant companions.

To amuse himself, Samson decided to tell them a riddle. Then he wagered each of his young Philistine companions a piece of fine linen and a change of fine clothing that none of them could answer his riddle by the end of the wedding feast. He declared, *Out of the eater came something to eat, and out of the strong came something sweet* (Judges 14:14). Of course, he was referring to the honey that came forth from the carcass of the lion. But three days later, his companions were still trying to solve the riddle.

The young Philistines were so upset by Samson's challenge that they threatened his new wife, saying, "Trick your husband into telling us what the riddle means, or we'll set fire to your father's house with you in it."

Naturally, she was terrified by their threats. She burst into tears before Samson and cried, "You don't really love me, or you would tell me the answer to your riddle."

Samson told her, "Look, I haven't even told my father or mother the answer to this riddle. Why should I tell you?"

Now, I want to point out two more weaknesses which often plagued Samson's life. First, he confided in people in whom he never should have confided. And, second, he let people badger him until they wore down his resolve and pressured him into doing things he really did not want to do.

Samson's wife cried and argued until he finally revealed to her the meaning of the riddle. Then she immediately told his Philistine companions, and they reported the answer back to him.

Samson was furious when he discovered that his wife had betrayed him. The Bible says that the Spirit of the Lord came upon him, and he killed thirty Philistines from another town, stripped them of their fine clothing, and gave their clothes to the men who had answered his riddle. Then he left his wife at her father's house and went back home in a huff.

Later, after he had cooled off, Samson decided to take a present to his wife to see if he could smooth things over (Judges 15). Actually, he wanted to spend the night with her, but her father informed him that he had already given her to Samson's best man. What a strange twist! Then he offered to give Samson one of his other daughters to be his wife, but Samson wouldn't hear of it.

He flew into such a violent rage that he went out and trapped three hundred foxes, tied their tails together in pairs, and stuck torches into the knots. Then he lit the torches and drove the foxes through the Philistines' cornfields. Not only did the fire ravage the corn crops, but also it torched the vineyards and olive trees.

When the Philistines found out that Samson had attacked them to avenge himself for his father-in-law's actions, they got the girl and her father and burned them to death. But that only outraged Samson further. So he attacked and killed some more Philistines, then fled and hid in a cave.

Remember, the Bible says the hand of the Lord was moving behind the scenes to stir up a war between Samson and the Philistines. You see, God wanted to use Samson to set His people free. And that tells me that He can use some very unexpected circumstances to cause His will to come to pass in your life. The key is for you to keep your heart pure and your spirit sensitive to Him. Then He can use even the most unusual circumstances to give you an outstanding victory.

So, don't allow the circumstances you're facing now to cause you to give up on God. The Bible tells us He can turn any situation around (Romans 8:28). What the devil means for evil, God can turn around for good (Genesis 50:20). A bad situation doesn't have to stay bad—especially when you reach out to God in faith and invite Him to help you.

Satan Doesn't Wear Us Down in a Single Day

Sometimes, the devil will add insult to injury when he's trying to stir up trouble in your life. That's what happened to Samson.

While Samson was in his hideout, the Philistines raided a town in Judah. When the men of Judah asked what had provoked the attack, the Philistines replied, "We've come to capture Samson and do to him what he did to us!"

Three thousand men from Judah tracked down Samson and demanded to know, "What have you done to us? Are you trying to destroy us? Don't you realize that the Philistines are our rulers?"

Finally, Samson agreed to let his countrymen take him captive, but he made them promise they wouldn't kill him. So they bound Israel's champion with heavy new ropes and delivered him to the Philistines. Just at that instant, God's power surged through Samson's body, and he snapped those ropes in two like they were made of thread.

I can imagine the Philistines recoiling with fear when they realized that Samson had broken free. I can hear them gasping in horror as he walked out into their midst, swinging the jawbone of a donkey as his only weapon, the fire of God flashing in his eyes. In a matter of a few moments, a thousand Philistines lay dead at Samson's feet.

Afterwards, Samson became extremely thirsty, and he cried out to the Lord for a drink of water. God opened a hollow place in the jawbone, causing a stream of water to gush forth, and Samson's spirit was revived as he drank.

Here was Samson, a man who had witnessed the awesome miracle-working power of God in action, a man who was greatly gifted of the Lord. He was walking knee-deep in miracles! How could such a man sink to the depths to which he sank?

More importantly, how can you and I resist Satan's traps so we don't follow in Samson's footsteps? Or, if you've already slipped and stumbled in some area of your life, how can you find your way back to the right path?

Remember, Satan doesn't wear us down in a single day. Most of the time, he doesn't drag us down into a pit overnight. Usually, he tries to lead us slowly down a path toward trouble. And many times, we help him by not taking time daily with God in prayer, His Word, and worship. As we keep walking in the wrong direction, away from God's will for our lives, Satan finds it easier to lead us into trouble.

Satan began to chisel away at Samson's character a little bit at a time. Perhaps he built up Samson's ego by telling him what a great man he was—what a powerful, manly warrior. Maybe he appealed to Samson's fleshly pride. Of course, he constantly eroded his judgment concerning women. As Satan played a tune, Samson began to dance.

First, the devil lured him into the bed of a prostitute in the city of Gaza (Judges 16). When the Philistines learned that Samson was there, they locked the gates of the city. But once again, the Spirit of the Lord came upon him, and he ripped the massive gates off their hinges and carried them to the top of the hill overlooking Mount Hebron.

Later, Samson met a Philistine woman named Delilah. She must have been a stunning beauty, full of feminine charms, because Satan used her to cast a spell upon the deliverer of Israel. Samson instantly fell in love with her, and his love cost him his life. The story of Samson's downfall is a reminder to us that it is crucial to get our weaknesses under control before they harm us permanently.

As soon as the five Philistine kings discovered that Delilah was Samson's new lover, they made a deal with her. They told her, "Trick him into telling you the secret of his strength so we will know how to overpower and bind him, and each of us will give you eleven hundred pieces of silver."

So Delilah began to quiz him. "Samson, what makes you so strong?" she pleaded, perhaps squeezing his muscles and playing up to his manly pride.

First, Samson teased and mocked her by giving her false answers. He told her, "If you tie me up with seven leather bowstrings, I'll be as weak as any other man."

So while he slept she tied him up with seven leather bowstrings, and then she cried out, "Samson, the Philistines are coming!" When he jumped up, he snapped those leather bowstrings as if they were mere strands of yarn.

Delilah was furious. "Samson, you've mocked me and told me lies," she said. "You've got to tell me your secret."

So he told her, "If you fasten me with new ropes, I'll be as weak as a kitten."

Again as he slept, Delilah eagerly wrapped new ropes around his arms and legs, and then she shouted, "The Philistines are coming!" But Samson awoke and flexed his muscles, and those ropes scattered in every direction. She might as well have bound him with a piece of ribbon.

Delilah really grew angry that time, yelling, "Samson, you've mocked me again. You've got to stop lying to me. I want to know the truth about your strength."

Then he told her, "If you weave the locks of my hair with a loom, I'll be as weak as any other man."

That night while he was asleep, Delilah braided the seven locks of his hair and wove them upon her loom. Then she called to him, "Samson, the Philistines are upon you," but he jerked his hair out of her loom in one split second.

At last Delilah began to cajole him mercilessly. "Samson, how can you say you love me, when you won't confide in me? This is the third time you've made a fool of me. Why won't you tell me the secret of your great strength?" She nagged him day after day until *he was tired to death* (Judges 16:16 NIV). She finally wore him down. Oh, how Satan loves to wear us down! When we get weary in our well-doing, that's when the devil can trip us up.

The Bible says that Samson finally spilled his guts to her. He said, "I've been dedicated to God as a Nazarite from my birth, and my hair has never been cut. If my hair were cut, I would lose all of my strength."

When Delilah realized that Samson had finally told her the truth, she sent for the Philistines. They rushed over and paid her the money they promised her. Then she lulled Samson to sleep with his head on her lap and called in a Philistine barber to shave off the seven braids of Samson's hair.

When the first rays of sunlight streaked through the curtains the next morning, Delilah whispered, "Wake up, Samson! The Philistines are here to capture you." Samson roused himself and thought, *I'll shake myself free as I've done so many times before.* But the Bible says he didn't know that the Spirit of the Lord had departed from him (Judges 16:20).

When Samson flexed his muscles that day, there was no strength in them. His arms fell limp at his sides. Suddenly the champion of God stood helpless before his enemies.

How Can We Resist the Lures of the Devil?

The irony of Samson's story is that he could have won so easily against Delilah. All he had to do was walk in the Spirit instead of walking in the flesh. Galatians 5:16 says, *Walk in the Spirit, and you shall not fulfill the lust of the flesh.*

This should have been no difficult battle for a man who could crush a thousand Philistines with the jawbone of a donkey or tear the gates of a great city off their hinges and drag them up a hill-side. The battle isn't hard for you and me if we'll use our spiritual weapons, if we'll draw upon the unfailing resources of the Holy Spirit when we need to fight against temptations.

How can we resist the lures of the devil? First of all, Romans 8:1–14 tells us we must learn to walk in the Spirit and refuse to pursue the things of the flesh. We must sow our seeds to the Spirit instead of sowing seeds to the flesh. In other words, we've got to fill our lives with the things of God—with prayer, with the Word, and with godly fellowship—instead of the things of this world.

It's a spiritual law: what you feed on is what will grow in your life. Galatians 6:8 puts it this way: *He who sows to his flesh will of the flesh reap corruption, but he who sows to the Spirit will of the Spirit reap everlasting life.* If you feed on the things of the Spirit, the urges of your flesh will grow weaker and weaker. On the other hand, if you feed on the things of the flesh, they will get a deadly grip on you. You can't afford to play around with sin.

Run from Temptation

Delilah represents anything that gets its hooks into us and causes us to let it have mastery over us. I tell you, don't just walk away from your Delilah. Run! Whatever temptation you're facing, flee from it. Fall upon the mercy of the Lord. Tell God, "I can't handle this by myself, but I know Your Spirit can help me cast it out of my life."

The Philistines pounced upon the mighty deliverer of Israel, shackled him, and gouged out his eyes. Then they led him away to the city of Gaza, where they threw him into prison. There Samson labored day after day in darkness, hitched up like a beast of burden to a grindstone and forced to grind in a mill. Can you see God's champion—blind, defeated, whipped, a prisoner? Dear Lord, please help us not to become prisoners of the devil!

No matter what traps we may stumble into, God is still a good God. The Bible teaches us that He doesn't give up on us, and that He answers us when we call on Him in faith. You can get up again—in faith—and you can move forward with the Lord, even after a terrible failure. Judges 16:22 says that Samson's hair began to grow back. No doubt as he trudged his wearisome path, around and around, grinding in the prison house, one day he must have felt something tickling his neck. When he reached up, he discovered that little wisps of hair were beginning to grow again. Praise God, when Samson felt that hair on his neck, he knew God's power was coming back into his life.

One day the Philistines decided to hold a great feast for their god, Dagon, to celebrate their victory over Israel's fallen champion. Someone chimed in, "Let Samson make sport for us!" All the lords and ladies gathered in the temple of Dagon for a great party. They were laughing and drinking and having the time of their lives when a soldier brought Samson from the prison to entertain them.

But they made a fatal mistake that day. They made Samson stand between the pillars that supported the temple. Samson asked the boy who was leading him to put his hands on the pillars, saying, "I need to lean on them."

The temple was jammed to the rafters as the Philistines shouted praises to their god. Amid the cheers and celebration, they began to jeer at Samson and mock the God of Abraham, Isaac, and Jacob.

As Samson leaned upon the pillars, he bowed his head and cried out, "O Lord God, remember me, I pray. Strengthen me just this once, that I may be avenged of my enemies for the loss of my two eyes." He was saying, "Lord, just let me feel Your power so I can deliver Israel one more time."

Samson prayed, "Let me die with the Philistines." And suddenly, like a great burst of wind, the Spirit of God blew through Samson's body, and his arms became like bands of steel. He flexed his muscles as he leaned into the pillars with all of his might, and the building trembled. Then the Spirit of God touched that cold stone, and the pillars began to pop and crack. Great pieces of plaster crashed to the ground as the stones dislodged and the temple shook and shuddered.

When Samson yanked those pillars out of their sockets, the walls cracked and heaved, and down they came. The temple of Dagon collapsed upon the hissing, jeering Philistines and buried every last one of them beneath the rubble. The great pillars of the temple fell upon Samson too, but he killed more Philistines in his death than he had killed during his entire lifetime.

If You Make a Mistake, Ask for Forgiveness

If you've come under the devil's attack, that doesn't mean it's because you've done something wrong or fallen into sin like Samson did. But if you have found yourself in trouble because of your own faults and shortcomings, God can still visit you once again with His miracle-working power. He can sweep over your life with the mighty, rushing wind of His Spirit. The answer is to call upon His Name. Ask Him to forgive you, and turn from the things that have bound you in the past. Remember, 1 John 1:9 says, *If we confess our sins, He is faithful and just to forgive us our sins and to cleanse us from all unrighteousness.*

Just like Samson, you can cry out to God for His power again in your life, and you can move ahead into new victories with Him. It just takes a willing, humble heart to ask God for forgiveness. And when you do, just wait and see what He does for you in your life!

CHAPTER 7
LISTEN TO THE GOOD REPORT

We're living in a time of great challenges in the world around us. Natural disasters are affecting the world in unprecedented numbers. You can hear and see bad news on your television set, radio, and the Internet any time of the day or night. Wherever you look, it may seem as if you're being bombarded by bad reports. And one tool the devil uses to try to trip us up is to get us focused on those bad reports, especially if they affect you personally. But the only way to make it through the hard situations you're going through is to listen to the good reports.

In Numbers 13–14, the Bible paints a vivid picture of a group of people who listened to the bad report, and it cost them dearly. After Moses led the children of Israel out of Egyptian bondage, there remained only an eleven-day journey to the Promised Land. But by the time the people had murmured and complained their way across the wilderness, it took them forty years to make the trip. Why did it take them so long? Because they listened to the bad report!

Here's what happened: After the Israelites escaped from Pharaoh's armies, they crossed the wilderness until they stood at the edge of the Promised Land. Then the Lord told Moses to send twelve of his men—a leader from each tribe—to spy out the land. When the spies returned, ten of them brought back alarming news (Numbers 13:33). They said, "There are huge giants in the land! They're so gigantic that we were like grasshoppers in their sight."

As soon as the travel-weary Israelites heard this bad report, consternation swept through the camp. They wept and wailed so loudly that Moses could scarcely quiet them down. Really, they were furious with him for leading them to a land filled with giants.

Never mind the fact that the spies brought back enormous clusters of grapes, huge pomegranates, and juicy figs from the rich countryside. Actually, the bounty of the land was staggering. But the ten spies who delivered the bad report were focused on the people who lived in the land—the "giants" they thought they couldn't defeat.

Then the other two spies, Joshua and Caleb, began to protest. "Don't be dismayed," they said. "Yes, we saw how tall the giants were, but the land is a wonderful land of plenty. The Lord is with us, and with His help, we're well able to go up and possess it!"

Joshua and Caleb's good report made the children of Israel boiling mad—so mad that they talked about stoning them (Numbers 14:6–10).

The most amazing thing to me about this whole story is the fact that all twelve spies searched out exactly the same piece of land. They all saw the same giants. Each one of them encountered the same obstacles. They all saw exactly the same clusters of grapes, the same bountiful fruit of the land.

Nothing about the land had changed between the time Joshua and Caleb searched it out and the time the rest of the spies searched it out. It was the very same land.

Why did the ten spies bring back such a totally different report from the one Joshua and Caleb brought back? It's very simple. The men who brought back the bad report were operating in fear, but Joshua and Caleb were operating in faith.

When the giants of life loom up before you and you feel so small in their sight, I hope you'll remember this story. You see, you can quiver and quake and repeat the bad report, or you can choose to face the giants in faith. Joshua and Caleb chose to face their enemy with their faith. They said, *The Lord is with us: fear them not* (Numbers 14:9 KJV).

Just think about the awful penalty the children of Israel paid because they listened to the bad report. They wandered through the wilderness for forty years until every last one who had believed the bad report was dead.

Think about it. When they listened to the bad report, it turned an eleven-day journey into a forty-year wilderness experience—and they never entered into the land, which represented their full victory. God had more for them than a wilderness experience, but because of their refusal to stand in faith, they never received God's best. I don't know about you, but I'll take the eleven-day journey and God's best for my life any day.

The Promised Land Belongs to You

Perhaps there is an area of your life in which you have received both a good report and a bad report. The question is, whose report are you going to believe?

There's a Promised Land stretching out before you, and it's divinely ordained to be yours. Your name has been stamped upon it from the beginning of time. God Almighty has chosen you to go up and possess the land. But you've got to listen to and believe the good report. You've got to give heed to the report of the Joshuas and Calebs of this life. You've got to listen to the good news of God's Word.

Through God, we are well able to possess the land! We are well able to take our cities for the Lord. We are well able to take our families, our neighborhoods, our schools, and our workplaces. I believe it's time for us to set our course for the Promised Land. We can prevail against the gates of hell and possess God's promises, if we'll only listen to the good report.

CHAPTER 8
YOUR FAITH CAN MAKE A GIANT FALL

First Samuel 17 tells of a battle between two armies—the army of the Philistines and the army of the living God. It's a battle between the Lord's champion and the devil's champion—a battle between a nine-foot-tall giant and a teenage shepherd who was almost totally unarmed.

This isn't merely a story that took place thousands of years ago. It's so up-to-date that it could have appeared in the newspaper today. This is the kind of battle that is being waged in the lives of people everywhere. Underdogs face overwhelming odds all the time. And maybe you feel like your circumstances are so overwhelming that there's no way to beat the odds. But I encourage you to let David's underdog victory build up your faith for miracles.

Picture this scene: On one side of the valley was the camp of the Israelites, where King Saul and all of his soldiers were huddled in fear around their campfires. On the other side of that great valley was the camp of the Philistines, where the undisputed champion of the day, a giant named Goliath, roared his threats at Israel's soldiers day and night.

For forty days Goliath strutted back and forth, bellowing out his message: "Send me a man to fight!" I mean, he had reduced the fight from a battle between two armies to a fight between two men. "If he defeats me," he yelled, "we'll be your slaves. But if I defeat him, Israel will serve the Philistines."

When King Saul and his armies heard Goliath's threats, they shook with intimidation and lost their courage. Even King Saul himself lost heart. Why? Because they were paralyzed with fear. And if the devil has another name, it's fear.

Now, let me take you across the miles to another scene on the hillsides of Bethlehem, where a young shepherd named David got a call from his father to take provisions to his older brothers who were serving in the army on the front lines with King Saul (1 Samuel 17:17–20).

When David arrived at the Israeli army camp, he heard Goliath shouting out his blasphemies at the armies of the living God, and he saw the giant swaggering back and forth across the valley. Not a single man of Israel was standing up against the giant. David whirled around to the soldiers standing nearby. "Is there not a cause?" he cried. "Isn't there somebody who will take on this godless Philistine?"

His brothers were furious when they heard his words, thinking he was trying to show them up. The eldest brother said accusingly, "We know you're just trying to get attention."

When word of David's boldness reached King Saul, he summoned the young man before him and looked him up and down. Then David volunteered to take on the giant.

"Son," Saul said, "that giant is nine feet tall and armed for battle! How on earth could you hope to take him on and come out alive? Why, have you seen his spear? It's massive! He's been a warrior from his youth, and you're so young!"

And it seems that way sometimes in our own lives too, doesn't it? The odds may appear overwhelming. Maybe no one is supporting us. But our faith is telling us to keep believing God for victory.

With his faith in God at the forefront of his mind, David reassured Saul, saying, "Sir, when I was tending my father's flocks, one day a lion leaped out of the woods and snatched one of my lambs, and a bear also charged the flock. I yanked that lion to the ground by his beard and killed him, and then I tore the bear limb from limb with my bare hands. The same God who delivered me out of the paws of the lion and the bear will deliver me from this godless Philistine."

No doubt King Saul was surprised by David's answer. After a few moments, he must have shrugged his shoulders and said something like, "Well, you don't look the part, but you certainly do sound the part!"

Then Saul added, "David, before you go, please put on my armor. Take my sword and my shield—all the weapons I would use if I were personally going into battle" (1 Samuel 17:38–39). In other words, King Saul was willing to give David his full suit of armor because he wasn't willing to use it himself. He was hiding from the giant in the shadow of the mountain.

David refused Saul's offer. In essence, he replied, "O King, this isn't a battle between flesh and blood. This isn't a fight with earthly weapons. This is God's battle! *And it's not by might, nor by power, but by God's Spirit that I'll win this fight!"* (See Zechariah 4:6.) You see, David realized that with God's help, he could defeat what seemed like an unbeatable enemy. And I believe you can too, as you stand in faith that God is with you and well able to help you overcome.

The hellish battle that you're embroiled in right now—the battle against sickness, against the enemy's onslaught against your children, your marriage, or your finances—that battle is the Lord's. Yes, you may be in a conflict, but it's not your fight. The Lord will fight for you, for the battle is His.

Goliath Collides with God's Miracle Power

I can picture Goliath standing in the middle of the valley, intimidating as he casts an enormous shadow across the hillsides. David knew the pressure was on. The future of Israel was hanging in the balance. But the Bible says that he ran to meet Goliath. I can imagine him whispering to himself, *Yea, though I walk through the valley of the shadow of death, I will fear no evil: for God is with me. His rod and His staff they comfort me* (Psalm 23:4 KJV).

David had his shepherd's stick in one hand and his slingshot in the other. And he was talented with that slingshot. He had practiced with it since he was a boy, and he knew exactly how to slide a stone into the sling. He knew the proper angle to throw it and the right moment to release it. And he also knew that when he released the stone, he had to release his faith to God.

I can picture David taunting Goliath and waving his staff at him, drawing the giant's attention away from the slingshot that was tucked away behind his back. I believe David had a firm grasp of military strategy, and he was merely coaxing Goliath to let his defenses down.

The giant sneered at him, "What am I, a dog, that you come at me with a stick?" Then he cursed David and added, *"Come to me, and I will give your flesh to the birds of the air and the beasts of the field"* (1 Samuel 17:44).

But David shouted back at him, *"You come to me with a sword, with a spear, and with a javelin. But I come to you in the name of the Lord of hosts, the God of the armies of Israel, whom you have defied. This day the Lord will deliver you into my hand, and I will strike you and take your head from you. And this day I will give the carcasses of the camp of the Philistines to the birds of the air and the wild beasts of the earth, that all the earth may know that there is a God in Israel. Then all this assembly shall know that the Lord does not save with sword and spear; for the battle is the Lord's, and He will give you into our hands"* (vv. 45–47).

Goliath must have raised the visor on his headgear to get a better look at the youth who was darting toward him, waving a stick in the air. But as soon as he lifted his visor, his forehead was exposed.

It was probably the only vulnerable spot on his body, and when he shoved his visor back to mock David, he exposed that vulnerable spot for everybody to see.

While Goliath was standing there with his defenses down, jeering at the young shepherd who was coming at him with a stick, David was busy loading his slingshot. He had his eyes fastened on the exposed spot on Goliath's forehead, and he began to swing that slingshot around and around.

Like a shot, David's stone catapulted from its socket. As it whizzed through the air, no doubt he was saying, "Lord, as I release this stone, I'm releasing my faith to You. Show everyone here who's bigger—this human giant, or You who created the universe."

That stone went hurtling through the air, and it struck Goliath in the forehead. The giant sank to the ground. The force of the blow merely dazed him, so David took Goliath's own sword—a big, long blade—and killed him with it and cut off his head.

The armies of Israel began to cheer wildly as they chased the Philistines all across that valley, cutting off their heads, and strewing their bodies on the ground for the fowls of the air to devour. Israel's enemies became their slaves because David realized that his godly spirit and obedience to the Lord were the keys to overwhelming victory and deliverance.

The Lord of the Universe Will Fight for You

The story of David and Goliath is more than just a story. It's a pattern for you and me to follow when the enemy comes against us—not to strike people physically, but just like David, we can stand up against overwhelming odds and declare in faith, "The battle is the Lord's. And in the Name of Jesus Christ of Nazareth, I will not stay trapped in the middle of this awful situation. I will walk through the valley of the shadow of death until I get to the light of deliverance on the other side. And I refuse to put up with this satanic attack any longer!"

I'm sure it looked absolutely ridiculous in the natural for David to take on that towering giant, armed with only a slingshot and his shepherd's staff. And some people may think it looks just as ridiculous for you or me to try to take on a great big giant of a problem, armed with only our Bibles and our faith.

But remember, no human understanding or wisdom can match your godly spirit, your faith, and your obedience. Remember also, the Lord of the universe is the One who fights for you. It's not by might, nor by power that you can win your battle. It's the Spirit of the Lord who puts the enemy to flight.

CHAPTER 9

WHAT TO DO WHEN TROUBLE COMES SUDDENLY

In 2 Chronicles 20, King Jehoshaphat was attacked by three enemy nations. The armies of the kings of Ammon, Moab, and Mount Seir declared war on Jehoshaphat and were threatening to destroy every living thing in Israel.

When word reached Jehoshaphat that a great multitude was coming against him from beyond the Dead Sea, he was terrified. In other words, he was a normal human being just like you and me, who felt scared when trouble came—especially when he wasn't expecting to find himself in the middle of a war with three enemies. Naturally, he felt fear grip him. But before Jehoshaphat made a move, the Bible says that he *set himself to seek the Lord* (2 Chronicles 20:3).

Notice that he didn't call on all of his counselors and wise men first. He didn't ask his top military aides to devise a strategy. Before he consulted anyone else, he cried out to God for help.

Let me ask you a question today. In the midst of whatever you're going through right now, while Satan is roaring his threats at you, are you seeking the Lord?

The Bible says that Jehoshaphat "set himself." Eagles have a way of setting their wings so that when the wind howls and beats against their feathers, they can soar above the storm. And Isaiah 40:31 declares that if we seek the Lord and we wait upon Him, we, too, shall renew our strength and mount up with wings like eagles.

The next thing Jehoshaphat did was call upon the whole nation to join him in seeking God. Second Chronicles 20:4 declares, *So Judah gathered together to ask help from the Lord.*

Now, I want you to picture this scene with the eyes of your spirit. Jehoshaphat and the people of God were no match for the armies marching toward them. In the natural, there was no way they could survive the attack. But the children of Israel were familiar with those kinds of odds, and they believed in their God!

I want you to hear with the ears of your spirit what Jehoshaphat said in verse 6. He cried out, "*O Lord God of our fathers, are You not God in heaven?*" In other words, he was saying, "God, You have not fallen off the throne. Even though our enemies have set themselves in array against us, we know that You're still God."

Then the king said, "*Do You not rule over all the kingdoms of the nations?*" He was saying, "God, aren't You the One who is still in control?" Next he added, *"And in Your hand is there not power and might, so that no one is able to withstand You?"*

We may sometimes feel as if the devil's forces outnumber God's forces, but when Satan fell, he took only one-third of the angels with him. That means there are still two-thirds of the angels who are on assignment in our behalf. Those who are with us are more than those who are with our enemy.

In verse 7, Jehoshaphat continued: "*Are You not our God, who drove out the inhabitants of this land before Your people Israel, and gave it to the descendants of Abraham Your friend forever?*" In other words, "Didn't You drive out the inhabitants so the children of Israel might have their inheritance—the Promised Land? If You gave it to us, then surely no enemy has the authority or power to take it away from us."

I love what Jehoshaphat said next. He declared, *"If calamity comes upon us, whether the sword of judgment, or plague or famine, we will stand in your presence before this temple that bears your Name and will cry out to you in our distress, and you will hear us and save* us" (v. 9 NIV). He was saying, "God, if our enemies give us trouble, we're going to run to You, and You will deliver us. We trust You."

If I could drive home one thought to you today, it would be this: God loves it when His children run to Him with their needs, believing in faith that He will help us. When it looks as if your life is falling apart at the seams and problems are coming at you from every direction, you can run to God for help and shelter.

What a declaration of faith Jehoshaphat made that day! He said, "God, we're going to run to You, and we believe You're going to save us." No ifs, ands, buts, or maybe sos. It was his faith that was doing the talking. And your faith is your victory, in Jesus' name.

Then he went on to plead his case before the Lord. In verses 10–11, Jehoshaphat said, *"And now, here are the people of Ammon, Moab, and Mount Seir—whom You would not let Israel invade when they came out of the land of Egypt, but they turned from them and did not destroy them—here they are, rewarding us by coming to throw us out of Your possession which You have given us to inherit."*

In other words, the king was saying, "Look, God, You wouldn't let us invade these nations or destroy their armies. Now they're coming to throw us out of the land that You have given us. That's not right!"

Is that the way you feel sometimes? Do you feel as if you've been obedient to the Lord and He has given you something, but now the devil is doing his best to tear it away from you? Then you need to keep on reading and see what Jehoshaphat did to bring a great deliverance into his life.

Praise Has the Power to Deliver You

Next, Jehoshaphat cried out to the Lord, *"O our God, will you not judge them? For we have no power against this great multitude that is coming against us"* (v. 12). Isn't that how it feels when the devil comes against you? You may feel as if you have no might and no strength when he sends his satanic onslaught ripping through your life. You may feel overwhelmed by the size of the problem that you're facing. You may not have any idea what to do.

If that's you, pay close attention to what Jehoshaphat said next: "*Nor do we know what to do, but our eyes are upon You.*" Jehoshaphat was saying, "God, we don't have well-trained military forces to take on this vast enemy. We don't have superior firepower. God, unless You tell us what to do, we're sunk!"

In verse 14 the Bible says that the Spirit of the Lord came upon one of the men who had gathered around Jehoshaphat to pray. In other words, Jehoshaphat asked for an answer and God gave him one. James 1:5 says, *If any of you lacks wisdom, let him ask of God, who gives to all liberally and without reproach, and it will be given to him.* You see, God never minds it when we ask for help.

Now, it's important to realize that when we hear God's reply to Jehoshaphat, the Bible gives us the man's credentials. It says, *Then the Spirit of the Lord came upon Jahaziel the son of Zechariah, the son of Benaiah, the son of Jeiel, the son of Mattaniah, a Levite of the sons of Asaph, in the midst of the assembly.*

Why do you suppose this Scripture gives us so much information about this particular man? Because God wants us to know something about the people who give us a word from the Lord. If someone you've never met before walks up to you and gives you a word about your life and it doesn't confirm something that God has already spoken in your heart, put it aside. If it's truly from God, it will come to pass as you obey God.

The Scripture tells us that this man, Jahaziel, was not only a Levite, a member of the priestly tribe, but he was also a descendant of Asaph, who was King David's own praise and worship leader. Jahaziel was a priest unto the Lord, a minister of God; and when he spoke a word by the Spirit, the people had every reason to believe that it was true. In other words, he had a previous track record.

Jahaziel said, "*Listen, King Jehoshaphat and all who live in Judah and Jerusalem! This is what the Lord says to you: 'Do not be afraid or discouraged because of this vast army. For the battle is not yours, but God's. Tomorrow march down against them. They will be climbing up by the Pass of Ziz, and you will find them at the end of the gorge in the Desert of Jeruel. You will not have to fight this battle. Take up your positions; stand firm and see the deliverance the Lord will give you, O Judah and Jerusalem. Do not be afraid; do not be discouraged. Go out to face them tomorrow, and the Lord will be with you'"* (vv. 15–17 NIV).

What a powerful word from God! Can you imagine how you would feel if you thought you were about to be wiped out by your enemies and the Lord said something like that to you? One of the most amazing things about this Scripture is the fact that the prophet told them the exact location of the enemy forces. And I believe God can reveal Satan's strategies to us in advance too.

When Jehoshaphat heard that word, he was so grateful and so in awe of God's goodness and mercy that he bowed his head with his face to the ground, and all the people of Judah and Jerusalem fell down in worship before the Lord. Then the Bible says that some of the Levites stood up and began to praise the Lord. It was a time of praise and worship, even before they saw God's victory come to pass.

Early the next morning, Jehoshaphat addressed the people, saying, *Believe in the Lord your God, so shall ye be established; believe his prophets, so shall ye prosper* (v. 20 KJV). That's a spiritual principle for your deliverance. When you receive a word from the Lord through one of His prophets, or even a word that God may speak in your own spirit, you need to latch on to that word by faith. Grab hold of it and believe, because your faith is what activates that word in your life.

If you're in a church service or you're attending a great healing crusade and a minister of the Gospel speaks a prophetic word, you can either receive that word as a personal word for your life, or you can let it float right by you. The choice is yours.

Jehoshaphat is saying, "If you believe the word that God's prophet speaks to you, if you accept it by faith and take hold of it in your life, you will prosper." On the other hand, if you let that word pass you by, it's not going to bring any success into your life.

What Jehoshaphat did next was highly unconventional. First of all, the Bible says that he consulted with the people before he sent them out into battle, and that's a most unusual thing for a king to do. I thank God for leaders who stay in touch with those they lead.

After he had consulted with the people, the king appointed praise and worship leaders to lead the army into battle. The Bible says, *Jehoshaphat appointed men to sing to the Lord and to praise him for the splendor of his holiness* (v. 21 NIV). The Amplified Bible says that the singers went out in their holy, priestly garments before the army, declaring, *Give thanks to the Lord, for His mercy and lovingkindness endure for ever!*

This is the most unconventional warfare I've ever heard of. Here is the Israeli army marching out to meet the armies of Moab, Ammon, and Mount Seir. Can you imagine those Israeli soldiers being led by a praise and worship team marching out in front of them? Now, that's unusual!

Psalm 22:3 says that God inhabits the praises of His people. I believe we've taken that Scripture far too lightly in the past. We simply haven't grasped how earthshaking it really is to praise the Lord.

Think about it for a moment. God Almighty—the Creator of heaven and earth—lives in, dwells in, and manifests His presence through our praises. That means all the supernatural forces of our God skyrocket into action when we praise Him. This is big! This Scripture is not talking about the sweet presence of the Lord settling over the congregation like a cloud. It's talking about our all-powerful Savior, the Lord of hosts, wiping out the devil's plan against us.

The People of God Didn't Have to Lift a Finger to Fight

When the sound of Israel's praises reached the ears of the Almighty, He set ambushes against the armies of Ammon, Moab, and Mount

Seir, and they were *smitten* (2 Chronicles 20:22 KJV). What does smitten mean? It means wiped out, annihilated.

Israel's enemies fell into such a frenzy that they began to turn upon each other and slaughter one another. When the men of Judah reached the battlefield, the Bible says, *They saw only dead bodies lying on the ground; no one had escaped* (v. 24 NIV).

Not only that, but Israel didn't have to lift a finger to fight. They simply had to obey God and march out to the battlefield. They just had to show up. And they had to praise the Lord, no matter how bleak things looked. God did the rest—and He did it perfectly.

The heaps of spoils were so vast that it took the soldiers three days to gather up all the abundance of valuables and precious jewelry. Thank God, Jehoshaphat didn't forget about the Lord as soon as He gave them the victory. The Bible says that after the men had finished gathering up the spoils, they assembled in the Valley of Berachah and began to shout loud praises unto God. Then Jehoshaphat led his army back to Jerusalem in a joyful victory march (vv. 25–27).

The fear of the Lord came upon all the surrounding nations when they heard how God had fought against the enemies of Israel and defeated them. *And the kingdom of Jehoshaphat was at peace, for his God had given him rest on every side* (v. 30 NIV). The Good News Translation of the Bible says, *Jehoshaphat ruled in peace, and God gave him security on every side.*

Isn't that what you want in your life—security on every side? I'm talking about the kind of security, safety, and peace that only God can give. When trouble comes into your life, don't let it dictate your relationship with God. Begin to praise the Lord, and expect His angels to give you security on every side.

CHAPTER 10

GOD IS GREATER THAN THE ODDS AGAINST YOU

Have you ever felt as if Satan was shooting his biggest guns at you and you couldn't find any place to hide? Or have you watched in horror as everybody around you seemed to collapse under his deadly barrage?

Isaiah 36 tells the story of a king of Israel named Hezekiah who must have felt exactly that way. You see, King Sennacherib of Assyria had already plundered the other great cities of Judah. Then he sent his messenger with a large army to Jerusalem to try to bully King Hezekiah into surrendering to him.

Just think about this scene for a moment. All the other cities in Judah had already fallen to the Assyrians. Why should Jerusalem be any different? Isn't that the way the devil comes against your life? Doesn't he try to tell you that things will go wrong for you, that you'll fail, and that God can't help you?

Don't you dare listen to the devil's threats! In Psalm 91:7 (NLT) the Lord said, *Though a thousand fall at your side, though ten thousand are dying around you, these evils will not touch you.* And Isaiah 54:17 (NIV) also declares, *No weapon forged against you will prevail.* Just take your stand on God's Word and expect God Almighty to deliver you.

King Hezekiah sent his men out to meet with King Sennacherib's messenger, and the man immediately began to rail at them. First he snarled, "Why don't you ask Hezekiah who he's trusting in?" Then he continued, "If you really think you're trusting in the Lord, then let me ask you one question. Why should God do anything for you, since Hezekiah is the one who knocked down all of His high places and altars and commanded the people to go to Jerusalem and worship the Lord?"

Oh, how the devil loves to come at you with a bunch of half-truths and make you doubt the decisions you've made to serve the Lord. Yes, Hezekiah did knock down the high places and altars throughout the land of Israel, but they were places of idol worship, not places where the people worshipped God.

In Isaiah 36:8–9, Sennacherib offered King Hezekiah a wager. He said, "If you can produce two thousand men in your army, I'll give you two thousand horses for them to ride." Then the messenger sneered, "With that tiny little army of yours, how can you possibly think about attacking even the smallest and worst contingent of our well-trained troops?"

Now, it was true that Hezekiah's armies were no match for the massive armies of Assyria. And it's true that in the natural, you're no match for the devil's assault against your life. The odds may be stacked against you. You may have received a shocking diagnosis of some incurable disease in your body. It may look as if your world has toppled upside down. Satan may have million-to-one odds against you, but our God can change the odds so fast that it will make the devil's head spin.

Notice Satan's next strategy. In Isaiah 36:10 the Assyrian messenger declared, "The Lord has sent me to destroy your land." All of a sudden, the devil himself is claiming to be on a mission for God. And the devil may try to tell you that too. He may want you to believe that sickness, poverty, or other troubles are the Lord's will for you. But 3 John 2 says that God wants you healthy and prosperous—spirit, soul, and body. So, don't believe the enemy's lies.

As soon as the messenger uttered those words, Hezekiah's men pleaded, "Why don't you speak in the Syrian language, since we understand it well? Don't speak in Hebrew because the people on the wall will hear you."

But that just egged him on. He began to shout in Hebrew, "My master wants everyone in Jerusalem to know that if you don't surrender, this city will be besieged until everyone is so hungry and thirsty that he will eat his own dung and drink his own urine."

Friend, the devil is a bully, and he loves to shout his tirades. First Peter 5:8 says that he goes about like a roaring lion. But he is not truly a lion. The only teeth he has are the teeth you give him when you believe in his threats more than you believe in the promises of God.

In Isaiah 36:14 the messenger shouted to the people of Jerusalem, "Don't let Hezekiah try to tell you that the Lord will deliver you! Have any of the gods of other nations delivered them from the king of Assyria?"

The messenger then told the people, "The king of Assyria says, 'If you'll surrender to me, I'll let each one of you have your own farm and garden and water. Then I'll make arrangements to take you to a land very much like your own—a land of corn and wine, a land of bread and vineyards.'" The devil is always ready to try to make a deal with you. He'll say, "If you'll just go along with this one issue, just bend a little here, be flexible there, it will go well with you." Pretty soon he'll strap a yoke of compromise around your neck, and you'll be wondering how on earth your life became such a mess.

I want you to notice how the people of Jerusalem responded to the threats and promises of the Assyrians. Verse 21 says, *They held their peace and answered him not a word; for the king's commandment was, "Do not answer him."* Thank God, they didn't try to carry on a conversation with their enemy. And don't you get into a conversation with your enemy (the devil) either! Don't try to argue with Satan. Begin to quote the Word of God instead, and watch him flee.

When Satan Attacks You, He's Attacking God

When Hezekiah's men reported to him what the messenger had said, he tore his clothes and covered himself with sackcloth as a sign of humility and mourning. Then he went into the temple to pray. You see, Hezekiah knew that his only hope was in the Lord.

At the same time, he sent his prime minister and the older priests with a message for the prophet Isaiah. In other words, not only did he seek the Lord in prayer but also he linked up his faith with a man of God. He told Isaiah: "This is a day of terrible trouble and distress, but perhaps the Lord has heard how the king of Assyria has scoffed at Him. Surely God won't let him get away with it."

Always remember that when Satan comes against your life, he isn't attacking just you. You're God's child, and that means he's also attacking God and His Word. When the devil comes against you, you have every right to say, "Lord, Satan is trying to make You look bad, but I don't believe You're going to let him get away with it!" That's what Hezekiah was saying.

After Isaiah had received the king's prayer request, he sent this message back to him: *This is what the Lord says: Do not be disturbed by this blasphemous speech against Me from the Assyrian king's messengers. Listen! I myself will move against him, and the king will receive a message that he is needed at home. So he will return to his land, where I will have him killed with a sword* (vv. 6–7 NLT). Isn't it wonderful to get a word from the Lord in the middle of a frightening situation?

Isaiah 37:9 says that Sennacherib received a report that the king of Egypt was marching out to attack him, so he quickly made plans to return home. But before he left, he dispatched a letter to King Hezekiah which was filled with more death threats.

The letter read, "Hezekiah, don't let your God deceive you when He says that Jerusalem will not be handed over to the king of Assyria. What makes you think your God will be able to deliver you when none of the gods of the other nations have been able to keep them from falling into my hands?" And he began to name a long list of all the other kings he had already crushed.

And isn't that exactly how the devil talks to you when you receive a word from the Lord? Doesn't he challenge what you believe you've heard from your heavenly Father? The devil still sings the same old song to you and me today.

Let's suppose for a moment that you've received a diagnosis of cancer in your body. Of course, the first thing Satan does is tell you that you're going to die. Then his next strategy is to bombard your mind with thoughts of other people who have died from cancer—especially good, Christian people!

Next he taunts you with the words, "What makes you think you're going to be any different?" He tries to convince you to doubt God's Word, to remove your faith from what God has said, because if he can get you to stop believing God, he can hinder you from receiving His promises in your life.

Listen to what God has to say about that! First of all, 2 Corinthians 10:12 says that we should not compare ourselves with others. Only God knows what happened in those cases where someone died an untimely death. But, really, the bottom line is this: Even if a terrible plague sweeps the entire globe, if you believe God's Word concerning healing, you can be the only person on earth who survives that plague. Your fate ultimately depends upon believing God and His Word.

You may say, "But, Richard, my father and mother both died of cancer." Thank God, their fate does not determine your fate! Yes, I realize that heredity does play a part in every person's health. But you have a choice. You can put your faith in what your heredity says about you, or you can put your faith in what God's Word says about you.

What does God's Word say about your health? Isaiah 53:5 (KJV) declares, *By His* [Jesus'] *stripes we are healed.* Matthew 8:17 says, *He Himself took our infirmities and bore our sicknesses.* And 3 John 2 (KJV) proclaims, *Beloved, I wish above all things that thou mayest prosper and be in health, even as thy soul prospereth.*

Your heredity may indicate that you are at a high risk to have a heart attack, cancer, diabetes, or some other devastating disease, and that is reality. I'm not talking about denying the facts here. Hezekiah didn't deny the fact that all the surrounding cities and nations had fallen to Sennacherib's armies. But he knew that God has a way of turning the devil's reality into a mighty victory for God's people.

As soon as Hezekiah read Sennacherib's letter, he went straight to the temple and laid the letter upon the altar before God. Then he lifted his voice in praise and worship and adoration to the Lord. He said, "O Lord, You alone are God of all the kingdoms of the earth. You made heaven and earth. Yet this arrogant Assyrian king has been mocking You, saying that You can't deliver Your people out of his hand.

"And, God, it's true that he's already conquered all the surrounding nations and overthrown their gods. But they weren't real gods anyway. They were gods made of wood and stone, fashioned by human hands." Then he pleaded with the Lord, "Deliver us from his hand so that all the kingdoms of the earth may know that You alone are God."

God didn't waste one second in answering Hezekiah's prayer. Isaiah sent him a message from the Lord, and it contained a strong word of rebuke for the Assyrian king, Sennacherib. The Lord said, "Sennacherib, you have raised your voice against Me, the Holy One of Israel. You have heaped insults upon Me. But because you rage against Me, I will put My hook in your nose and My bit in your mouth, and I will make you return by the way you came" (vv. 28–29). And that's exactly what the Lord is telling Satan in your behalf right now. He's telling the devil, "You're going to have to return by the way you came."

Then God told Hezekiah, "*Here is the proof that I am the one who is delivering this city from the king of Assyria: This year he will abandon his siege. Although it is too late now to plant your crops, and you will have only volunteer grain this fall, still it will give you enough seed for a small harvest next year, and two years from now you will be living in luxury again*" (Isaiah 37:30 TLB).

Thank God, He doesn't merely want to deliver us out of Satan's clutches. He wants to completely restore what the devil has stolen. He wants us to live in His abundance again.

God Doesn't Mess Around with Satan When Satan Messes Around with You

At the close of these powerful chapters from the book of Isaiah, God gives some of the strongest words the Bible records against an enemy of His people: "*He* [King Sennacherib] *shall not come into this city, nor shoot an arrow there, nor come before it with shield, nor build a siege mound against it. By the way that he came, by the same shall he return; and he shall not come into this city...for I will defend this city, to save it for My own sake*" (vv. 33–35).

You see, the Lord doesn't mess around with the devil when the devil messes around with you. He tells Satan, "I will defend them for My sake and for the sake of My Word."

Now, I want you to read what God did to those Assyrian forces: *Then the angel of the Lord went out and put to death a hundred and eighty-five thousand in the Assyrian camp. When the people got up the next morning—there were all the dead bodies* (Isaiah 37:36 NIV).

No doubt Sennacherib got the message. The Bible says that he immediately broke camp, fled to Nineveh, and stayed there. One day as he was worshipping Nisroch, his demon god, two of his own sons stabbed him to death right there in the house of his god. He died in his own land, just as the Lord had predicted.

I tell you, if you'll do what Hezekiah did when trouble comes and the odds seem to be against you... If you will refuse to believe the devil's lies, turn to the Lord in faith, and believe Him, He can rescue you from seemingly impossible odds. When you call upon the Lord in faith, when you lay Satan's threats upon the altar before God, you can expect Him to make the devil eat his words. You can expect to hear Him say, "Satan, you've got to go! Leave My child alone, and return by the way you came."

CHAPTER 11
TURNING THREATS INTO MIRACLES

In 1 Kings 19:4, the prophet Elijah was experiencing a time that had him so discouraged and down that he wished he could die. He had come under the attack of Jezebel, the wickedest queen ever known to Israel, and her death threats had sent him into a tailspin.

If you remember the background of this story found in 1 Kings 17, Elijah had told Jezebel's husband, King Ahab, "It's not going to rain until I say so." And as soon as he said those words, the Lord told him to flee for his life. First he camped beside a brook called Cherith, where he drank from the waters of the brook, and the ravens dropped meat down from the sky for him to eat. When the brook dried up and the ravens stopped flying by, the Lord sent him to a city called Zarephath where He had commanded a widow to sustain him.

When Elijah arrived at the widow's house, she was cooking her last supper. She told him, "I'm going to fry a couple of pancakes for my boy and me, and we're going to eat them and then starve to death because we have no food left."

Many people might have said, "God, You sure missed it this time. How can this widow feed me if she has no food?" But Elijah trusted in God, in spite of what things looked like. He was operating by the Spirit of God when he replied, "Give me a portion first."

Then Elijah gave her the clincher. He said, *For thus says the Lord God of Israel: 'The bin of flour shall not be used up, nor shall the jar of oil run dry, until the day the Lord sends rain on the earth* (vv. 13–14). Praise God, she obeyed Elijah, and the Bible says that they "did eat many days"— as long as it was needed—from that near-empty meal barrel and jar of oil.

When Pressure Comes, Push Back

While Elijah was hiding from King Ahab, the king ordered all of his spies and his secret service agents to comb the countryside to look for the prophet of God. You see, Ahab blamed Elijah for the terrible drought in Israel, but it had really been caused by Ahab and Jezebel when they refused to obey the Lord and led the people to worship Baal (1 Kings 16–19.)

When God finally sent Elijah back to town, he told Ahab to round up the four hundred and fifty prophets of Baal and the four hundred other Satanic prophets who ate at Jezebel's table so he could meet them face-to-face. All the people and the prophets gathered at Mount Carmel, and Elijah proclaimed, *"How long will you waver between two opinions? If the Lord is God, follow him; but if Baal is God, follow him." But the people said nothing* (1 Kings 18:21 NIV).

Then Elijah took two bulls, one for the prophets of Baal and one for himself to sacrifice to the Lord. He told them, "Cut your bull into pieces and lay it on the wood, but don't put any fire under it; and I'll do the same with mine. Then you call upon the name of your gods, and I'll call upon the Name of the Lord: and the God who answers by fire, let him be God."

The prophets of Baal carefully laid their bull upon the altar, and then they began to cry out to their god, Baal, all morning.

Around noon Elijah began to mock them, saying, "Perhaps your god is talking to somebody, or he is on a journey. Or maybe he's asleep and must be awakened." Well, that only made the prophets flail about even more. They jumped and shouted and cut themselves with knives until the blood gushed out, trying to convince Baal to send down fire. Then they began to prophesy, but absolutely nothing happened. The Bible says that *there was no reply, no voice, no answer* (1 Kings 18:29 TLB).

Meanwhile, about sunset, Elijah dug a trench around the altar and got the wood ready. Then he cut his bull into pieces and laid it upon the altar. Next, he ordered barrels to be filled with water and poured over the bull until the water sloshed all the way down the altar and filled the trench.

Elijah didn't cut himself or dance around the altar. He didn't jump and shout to see if he could get the Lord to answer him. Instead, he called upon the Name of his God in faith and confidence. He said, "*Hear me, O Lord, hear me, that this people may know that You are the Lord God*" (v. 37). And the fire of the Lord fell!

First, it consumed the bull upon the altar. Then the wood burst into flames, and the flames licked up all the water in the trench. When the people saw it, they immediately fell on their faces and cried out, "*The Lord, He is God! The Lord, He is God!*" (v. 39)

Next, Elijah told the people to seize the prophets of Baal and execute them, just as God had commanded them to do.

Then Elijah told Ahab, "Eat and drink, for I hear the sound of an abundance of rain. I hear thunder, and the thunder says that it's going to be a gully washer. The rain is going to come down in torrents. It's going to break the drought."

Elijah climbed to the top of Mount Carmel, the very peak of the mountain, got down on the ground, put his head between his knees, and began to cry out to God for rain. Then he sent his aide to look out across the Mediterranean Sea for a sign of a cloud.

When the man came back, he said, "There is nothing," but Elijah sent him six more times to look for rain. The seventh time, the aide exclaimed, "I see a little cloud the size of a man's hand coming out of the sea." I tell you, that cloud meant everything to Elijah.

He said, "Go tell Ahab to get his chariot ready, so the rain won't stop him." When Ahab heard that word, he jumped in his chariot, pulled by two of the fastest horses in Israel, and drove with all of his fury to Jezreel. Then, the Bible says, Elijah raced like the wind across the Plain of Esdraelon. As the rain pelted down, Elijah ran with all of his might, and he beat Ahab to the gates of the city.

When King Ahab told his wife, Jezebel, what Elijah had done—how he had killed all of her false prophets—she became enraged. She sent a message to Elijah that said: "I'm going to do the same thing to you that you did to my prophets!" She put out a death contract on him and told him, "By this time tomorrow you're going to be cold and in the grave" (1 Kings 19:1–2).

Elijah was attacked by Jezebel because he had been obedient to the Lord. When you're obedient to the Lord—when you praise Him, when you lead people to Jesus, when you pray for the sick and they are healed—Satan is not going to be happy about it. When you're doing the Lord's work, the devil will come after you to try to stop you. And he came after Elijah through Jezebel.

When Elijah read Jezebel's message, fear gripped him, and he fled into the wilderness to a place called Beersheba. It's a little spot way out in the desert, and it's very hot and dusty and desolate.

The Bible says that Elijah traveled a day's journey into the wilderness, sat down under a juniper tree, and began to cry out to the Lord. He said, "God, why don't You just let me die?" Most of us have probably felt discouragement like that at some time in our lives. Even Elijah wasn't exempt from that type of feeling.

As he slept, an angel came and touched him and said, *"Arise and eat"* (1 Kings 19:5). Elijah roused himself, looked around, and saw some food cooking on hot coals and a jar of water. Didn't the Lord say in Psalm 23:5 that He would prepare a table before you in the presence of your enemies? I believe God has prepared a table for you this very moment, even if you're in the midst of a serious trial of your faith.

Elijah ate and drank, then lay down again. After he had rested, the angel of the Lord touched him a second time and said, *"Arise and eat, because the journey is too great for you"* (v. 7).

Elijah wasn't aware that he was about to embark on a great journey for the Lord. All he knew was that he was lying under a juniper tree in the wilderness and he felt like dying. He had done everything according to the Word of God, but it had only produced a death contract on his life. He felt like quitting. He wanted to chuck the whole deal and escape to the farthest place on the face of the earth.

Next, the Bible says, *He arose, and ate and drank; and he went in the strength of that food forty days and forty nights as far as Horeb, the mountain of God* (v. 8).

So Elijah spent the night on Mount Horeb, hiding in a cave, wrapped in his mantle, searching for God. When the devil comes against you, that's the time for you to seek the Lord.

Then the word of the Lord came to the prophet Elijah that day and told him, "Go out and stand before Me on the mountain." When Elijah obeyed, the wind started to howl. You talk about a windstorm! The wind roared so hard that the rocks in the mountain began to break into pieces. Surely this must be the Lord talking to me, Elijah thought, but the Bible says that God wasn't in the wind.

Then the earth beneath his feet began to rumble and sway. Elijah felt the very footing upon which he was standing shake. And perhaps that's the way you feel today—as if the ground is shaking underneath you. Maybe you feel as if your faith and everything in your life is shaking underneath you. Elijah thought the Lord must be in the violent tremor, but the Bible says, *The Lord was not in the earthquake* (v. 11).

After the earthquake, a fire erupted, and the flames began to shoot upward into the sky. But the Lord wasn't in the fire either.

Then Elijah heard a still, small voice whispering to him, saying, "What are you doing here?" The lonely prophet wrapped his face in his mantle and began to rehearse his case before the Lord.

He said, "I have been very zealous for the Lord God of hosts. I have worked my heart out for You, Lord. All the rest of these people have forsaken Your covenant, thrown down Your altars, and killed Your prophets, and I'm the only one left. Now Jezebel is trying to kill me too!"

But God wasn't moved by Elijah's sad story. He asked him, "Why are you feeling so sorry for yourself? Why are you so upset because Jezebel wants to cut your head off?"

You see, there's always somebody who wants to stop the move of God in your life. There will be people who want to stop you from prospering, who want to stop you from experiencing the presence of the Lord in your life. But God said to Elijah, "Don't pay any attention to the Jezebels of life. Don't let your circumstances get to you. You have a great work to do for Me, so stop lying around in that puddle of tears. Get down off this mountain and do what I've commanded you to do."

God was saying, "Elijah, when the devil comes after you, don't give in to him. Don't get sidetracked. Just get on with your work for Me, because I have a great plan for your life!"

Elijah obeyed the voice of the Lord and went on about his business, which included anointing a young man named Elisha, who would someday take Elijah's place and do twice as many miracles in the Name of the Lord. And I encourage you to keep on doing what God has called you to do, because I believe He has great things in store for you too.

CHAPTER 12
WHEN THINGS GO FROM BAD TO WORSE

We live in a world where troubles may come at any time. And sometimes, things come at us so fast and furious that it's hard to cope. We may even think our circumstances have gotten as bad as they can get, only to see them grow worse. But in such times, God is still with us. And He can turn even the most devastating situations around for our good.

King David experienced such a time in his own life when he and his soldiers returned from a mission only to discover that the Amalekites had plundered the city of Ziklag and burned their homes to the ground (1 Samuel 30). Now, that's bad. But it didn't take long for things to go from bad to worse.

After David's men saw the smoldering rubble that had once been their homes, they also discovered that their wives and children had been taken captive. They burst into tears, and the Bible says that they wept so hard they couldn't weep anymore. Then they became angry and picked up stones to kill David.

When David faced Goliath, he faced an enemy who came at him from the ranks of the Philistines, from outsiders. But now he was facing opposition from within his own ranks, from insiders. Some six hundred of David's own choice soldiers had turned against him. His own people were ready to take David's life in their hands because they had lost it all, and they blamed him for it.

Does that describe your situation today? Perhaps you feel as if you've lost everything, and maybe the people who normally support you have turned against you. But notice this: David didn't buy the devil's lie that when things go from bad to worse, they automatically have to end in destruction. He believed that God would turn bad and worse into a miracle! I want to share with you some powerful steps David took that caused him to receive his miracle.

David Encouraged Himself in the Lord

It's so wonderful when your friends and family shower you with words of encouragement. It's so comforting when you're down-and-out and somebody pats you on the shoulder and reassures you, saying, "Everything is going to be all right."

But what about the times when your friends and family shut you out? What about the times when the ones who are the closest to you seem to turn on you? What do you do when there's no one around to give you a kind word? When that happens, you have to encourage yourself in the Lord.

I'm not talking about giving yourself a nice little pep talk here. I'm not talking about the power of positive thinking either, although a great big positive dose of God's Word can do your thinking a world of good.

Some people try to encourage themselves by turning to alcohol, drugs, or some other form of unhealthy or addictive behavior. Even Christians sometimes try to numb themselves to the pain and trials of life through various unhealthy escape and defense mechanisms. But God has provided supernatural encouragement for our soul that far surpasses anything the world has to offer.

When David encouraged himself in the Lord, he must have begun to count his blessings, one by one. He must have thought about the supernatural way God had snatched him from the paws of both a lion and a bear (1 Samuel 17:37). He must have reminded himself of how he had triumphed over the giant Goliath, even though he was a virtually unarmed shepherd.

Perhaps David preached himself happy that day. Maybe he began to sing praise songs unto the Lord. No doubt he began to lift his voice to God in prayer. The Bible doesn't say exactly what he did to encourage himself in the Lord, but the bottom line is this: David let God help him get his spirit man to stand up on the inside.

Did you know that it's hard to receive a miracle from God when your spirit man is lying down? I'm talking about the real you on the inside. Maybe the devil has knocked the wind out of your sails. Perhaps he has stolen all of your possessions and robbed you of your family, your health, your peace, and your joy. Before you can recover it all, your spirit man needs to stand up tall in faith. That's why it's important to encourage yourself in the Lord.

David Inquired of the Lord

The second thing David did to get himself hooked up with God's miracle power was to ask God for wisdom. Thank God that we have a Savior we can run to when our life seems to be falling apart.

David asked the Lord, "What shall I do?" When you're struck down by health problems or your finances are wiped out, or your family seems to be falling apart or you're facing some other trouble, it's time to ask the Lord, "What shall I do?" I believe God has a supernatural plan of deliverance for your life. But you won't know what that plan is if you don't ask God to show it to you, if you don't take the time to wait on Him for His divine guidance.

Rather than trying to figure things out on his own, David went to the Lord for advice. He said, "Should we pursue this enemy that has plundered our city and carried away our wives and children, or should we just forget about the whole thing? Should we give up on this situation, or should we go after them in the Name of the Lord?" Thank God, the Lord had an answer for him! He said, "*Pursue, for you shall surely overtake them and without fail recover all*" (1 Samuel 30:8). I believe this is a word for all of us—because I believe God doesn't intend for us to give up and let the devil walk all over us. The Lord can help us overcome and receive whatever restoration we need, as long as we refuse to quit.

So, don't you dare run from the devil. When trouble hits your life, it's time for you to go to the Lord and put Satan on the run.

David and His Men Entered into a Faith Agreement

David found a third powerful way to activate God's miracle power in his life. He asked his men to enter into a faith agreement with him to help him recover all.

In Matthew 18:18–19 Jesus declared, "*Assuredly, I say to you, whatever you bind on earth will be bound in heaven, and whatever you loose on earth will be loosed in heaven. Again I say to you that if two of you agree on earth concerning anything that they ask, it will be done for them by My Father in heaven.*" Now, don't pass over this Scripture lightly. Jesus said, "*Assuredly,*" or, "I give you My assurance. I give you My word." Jesus promised that God, our heavenly Father, would back up our prayers of agreement. And when Jesus makes a promise, you can count on it.

Here are five very important principles about the prayer of agreement that can help you receive your deliverance:

1. Before you enter into a prayer of agreement, make sure that your agreement is in accordance with the Word of God. What you're believing for has to be in harmony with the Bible. It can't be based upon some wish or whim or some vain imagination. What you're agreeing with is God and His Word.
2. You also need to know the person you're going into agreement with. Don't run to someone you hardly know and ask them, "Will you agree with me about this?" Instead, ask the Lord: "Heavenly Father, in the Name of Jesus, show me specifically who You want me to go into agreement with." I believe God will reveal that person to you.

I'm very careful about who I share my prayer requests with, because I don't want to give Satan a chance to destroy my prayer of agreement. If someone's faith isn't in agreement with yours, if they don't believe the same things about God's Word that you believe, how can they enter into an agreement with you? I mean, your faith can be built up so high and you can be standing on God's Word, but if you ask someone to agree with you who doesn't believe that part of the Word, they can dash your faith to pieces. It's important to find someone of like faith to agree with you.

3. The third thing you need to do is make sure you know what you're going into agreement for. The Bible teaches us to be specific with the Lord. Philippians 4:6 says, *Let your requests be made known to God.* And Isaiah 43:26 tells us, *"Put Me in remembrance; let us contend together. State your case that you may be acquitted."*

Plead your case before God. Tell Him specifically what you need. Remind Him of what His Word says about your needs, and make certain that whoever you're asking to agree with you understands exactly what you're agreeing for. If both of you are not believing for the same thing, it's hard for the prayer of agreement to work.

4. Before you go into agreement with someone, ask yourself these questions: What am I permitting in my life? Is there anything I need to stand against, in faith? Is there anything I need to put a stop to?

There's something important that I want you to notice about this Scripture in Matthew 18:18–19. The Good News Translation says, *What you prohibit* [stop] *on earth will be prohibited* [stopped] *in heaven, and what you permit on earth will be permitted in heaven.* Many times we desire the will of God, but our actions can stop it from happening. Other times we don't want certain bad things to happen, but our actions can permit them to happen. Another way to put it is this: Whatever you allow, God allows.

Maybe you're allowing things in your life that are unlike God. That can mean that you're making choices that are ungodly. But it can also mean you're allowing the devil to work by not using your faith to resist him. In either case, until you bind those things and remove them from your life, the path between you and your miracle will always be filled with traps and land mines.

5. One of the most important things I could ever say to you about the prayer of agreement is this: Once you enter into an agreement, don't come out of the agreement. Stick to it! It's like a legal contract. Before you enter into a legal contract, you carefully examine the fine print. You make certain that both parties are in harmony, because once that contract is signed, it becomes binding.

It's the same way with the Word of God. Once you come into agreement with God's Word for a miracle, don't come out of the agreement until the miracle comes.

A lot of people say, "Oh, yeah, I'll agree with you," and then they walk right out the door and say, "God, I wonder if that's going to come to pass." By doing so, they cancel out your prayer with their doubt and unbelief. Or suddenly the circumstances change, and poof—all of their faith seems to go up in smoke.

When you go into a prayer of agreement, you're bound by God's Word to stick to that agreement, regardless of the circumstances. If the outward circumstances frighten somebody or make them full of doubt, then they're not the right person for you to pray and agree with.

I encourage you to find scriptures that speak about what you're believing for, release your faith according to those scriptures, and then don't budge. Get hold of God's promise, grit your teeth, and don't be moved by your feelings or the circumstances. That's the kind of faith agreement that can produce miracles.

David Finished the Fight

Terrible questions plague the minds of many Christians when trouble comes their way. So many times, they don't feel like going on. But Jesus told us in Luke 9:62 to keep our hands on the plow. Galatians 6:9 says, *Let us not grow weary while doing good, for in due season we shall reap if we do not lose heart.*

Have you ever stopped to think that your level of victory is not determined by how big or how bad the devil's attack is? It's how you respond to his attack with your faith. You've got to fight the good fight of faith until you win.

Many times, Christianity is preached as a surface religion. People get the mistaken notion that you can just give your heart to Jesus, and then life is going to be all peaches and cream. They don't realize there is a devil on the loose on planet earth. There are opposing forces that don't want us to serve God and to be successful. And it's so easy to give up and quit believing God.

David and his men could have collapsed and given up hope in the middle of that heap of smoking ashes at Ziklag. Instead, they chose to fight. They fought their enemies until they won.

They crushed the Amalekites, and 1 Samuel 30:18 says that David recovered all that the enemy had carried away. The Amplified Bible says, *Nothing was missing, small or great, sons or daughters, spoil, or anything that had been taken; David recovered all. Also David captured all the flocks and herds [which the enemy had], and the people drove those animals before him and said, This is David's spoil* (1 Samuel 30:19–20). He came home with every single one of his possessions, all his people, plus the increase supplied by the enemy. He got back what he lost, with interest.

Now, isn't that the way you want to return home from your battles with Satan's forces? Not only can you recover everything he has stolen from you, but you can march home from the battle loaded down with the spoils of his kingdom. I believe that is God's victorious plan for your life.

CHAPTER 13
EMOTIONAL SURVIVAL IN A CRAZY, MIXED-UP WORLD

So many people today are tormented by gaping wounds from their past. They've been attacked or hurt by the people who were supposed to love them the most, and now they're floundering. They're trying desperately to wade through all the emotional baggage that has been handed down to them from previous generations.

When I think about the emotional turmoil that plagues so many people today, I'm reminded of the story of Joseph in the Bible. If anybody ever had a right to have an emotional problem, it was Joseph. Just look at his family background. Just consider some of their actions: Joseph's father, Jacob, stole the birthright and the blessing that rightfully belonged to his brother, Esau. His grandmother, Rebekah, helped Jacob cheat his brother out of the blessing (Genesis 27).

Then there were Joseph's brothers. They went to a town named Shechem one day and slaughtered all the men (Genesis 34:1–24). Even though a serious crime had been committed to provoke their anger, their response was a terrible overreaction because they killed all the men, even though some of them had done nothing wrong.

And you thought you had problems? Joseph's family was a bunch of outlaws.

On top of being haunted by his family background, Joseph was also the victim of his own brothers' cruelty. Joseph was his father's favorite son. Jacob loved him so much that he gave him a magnificent hand-woven coat of many colors (Genesis 37). Can you imagine what his brothers thought? The jealousy they must have felt?

Genesis 37:2 says that Joseph also brought bad reports to his father about what his brothers were doing. In other words, he was a tattletale. But he really pushed his brothers over the edge when he began to have big dreams about his future.

First, Joseph dreamed that he and his brothers were binding sheaves in the field, and his sheaf stood up while their sheaves bowed down to his. He couldn't wait to tell them about his dream, but they bristled because of his cocky attitude. And they hated him.

Later Joseph dreamed that the sun, the moon, and eleven stars (representing his father, mother, and eleven brothers) bowed down before him. Poor Joseph made the mistake of telling his brothers that dream too, and they nearly came unglued. His father even rebuked him for it, but the Bible says that Jacob pondered the dream in his heart.

One day Joseph's brothers herded their flocks to Shechem to graze, and Jacob sent Joseph to check on them. When he arrived in Shechem, there was no sign of his brothers or their flocks, but a man from the area told him they had gone to Dothan. So he went after his brothers and found them.

Perhaps the nightlife in Dothan was better than the nightlife in Shechem, or maybe the restaurants were more appetizing. I can just imagine how Joseph's wheels were turning as he rehearsed the story he was going to tell his father.

When his brothers saw him coming that day, they groaned in disgust. *Here comes that dreamer… Come on, let's kill him… Then we'll see what will become of all his dreams* (vv. 19–20 TLB).

Reuben, his oldest brother, finally convinced them to throw Joseph into a pit instead of killing him. The Bible says that he planned to come back later and rescue the boy.

But in the meantime, they stripped Joseph of his brightly-colored coat and shoved him down into a well. While they were eating dinner around their campfire, a caravan of traders rode past them in a cloud of dust. Judah got an idea. "Why don't we sell Joseph to the traders? Let's not kill him and have his blood on our hands. After all, he is our brother." And the brothers agreed. What a wonderful way to get rid of their thorn in the flesh—or so they thought.

Joseph was sold into slavery by his very own brothers. They took his prized coat, smeared it with the blood of a goat, and told their father that a wild beast had torn Joseph to pieces. The Bible says that Jacob refused to be comforted, and he mourned bitterly for his son.

That's a horrible story! Joseph was attacked and harmed by his own brothers, his own flesh and blood, the people who should have loved him and supported him the most.

There are many people today who are grappling with pasts so awful that it's almost impossible to imagine the ordeals they've endured. Every day we receive letters, emails, and phone calls from people who have been hurt by the very ones who should have loved them and nurtured them, and it breaks my heart.

But even if you have had problems like that in your past—perhaps during your childhood, perhaps from a former spouse or another loved one—the story of Joseph proves that you don't have to remain trapped by what happened to you. You can forgive those who have hurt you. You can release all that mess to God, and your future can be as bright as the dawn.

God Is With You in the Ups and Downs of Life

Joseph rose to prominence in the house of a man named Potiphar, a member of the staff of Pharaoh, the king of Egypt. And God caused Joseph to shine like a bright star in the land of Egypt. Potiphar was so amazed at the way God's hand was upon this young Hebrew that he turned the management of his own household and all of his lands over to Joseph. Genesis 39:5 says that God blessed the house of the Egyptian because of Joseph.

Naturally, the devil had a hissy fit when he saw how well Joseph was doing, so he decided to set a trap for him. The Bible says that Joseph was a handsome, well-built young man, and Potiphar's wife began to flirt with him. He always refused her advances, but that only made her mad and ruffled her pride. Day after day, she tried every trick she could think of to seduce Joseph, but he always turned her down.

Then one day when they were alone in the house, she pleaded with him once again to go to bed with her, and once again he refused. This time he actually ran from her presence, but as he did, she managed to grab his jacket.

When Potiphar returned home that day, his wife greeted him with a wild story she had concocted: "Your Hebrew slave tried to rape me, but when I screamed, he ran!" Then she flashed Joseph's jacket in front of Potiphar's eyes, and he became so furious that he had Joseph cast into prison.

Talk about ups and downs. That's the story of Joseph's life—and it must have caused him many a day of emotional struggle and disappointment.

Yet it's amazing to see how God's hand was still upon Joseph, even after he was thrown into jail. In a very short time, the warden had handed over the administration of the entire prison to Joseph. In fact, all the prisoners reported to him personally.

You may feel as if you've faced attacks from those who were the closest to you, and now the devil has cast you into a deep, dark pit. I declare to you from the Word of God that if you forgive those who have hurt you and put your trust in the Lord, you can expect Him to shine His light down into that pit and cause you to prosper right in the middle of your pain and loss. You can expect Him to turn that pit into a fruitful land.

Joseph Overcame His Obstacles Instead of Wallowing in Them

In Pharaoh's prison, Joseph had every reason to let his past consume him. He could have focused on his pain and nursed his hurts. He could have told his sad story to all the other prisoners. Instead, he kept his heart pure and refused to cling to bitterness, unforgiveness, or despair. As a result, God was able to turn around for Joseph's good what the devil meant for evil (Genesis 50:20). But at first, it sure didn't look like that was going to happen.

One day two prominent men suddenly wound up in jail with Joseph (Genesis 40). One was the king's chief butler, and the other was the king's baker. Joseph was given charge over both of these men. While in prison, they each dreamed an unusual dream. When they awakened, they were extremely troubled, so Joseph asked them what was bothering them. As soon as they told him about their dreams, he replied, *Interpreting dreams is God's business... Tell me what you saw* (Genesis 40:8 TLB).

Joseph's gift of interpreting dreams began to change his destiny again. And I believe God has given you certain gifts and talents too. If you will be faithful and develop those gifts, they can take you to places you never even dreamed of.

When Joseph interpreted the butler's dream, he told him he would be restored to favor with Pharaoh. But the baker's dream revealed that he was about to be executed. Then Joseph told the butler, "Remember me to Pharaoh when you're restored." However, as soon as the man was released, he forgot all about Joseph. Two more long, lonely years passed as Joseph sat there in prison, seemingly forgotten.

He could have felt sorry for himself and complained, "Look what I did for that butler, and he forgot all about me." He could have wallowed in self-pity. He could have blamed everybody else for his troubles. Surely he must have been tempted to let anger, bitterness, and unforgiveness control his behavior. But he chose to overcome those obstacles rather than wallow in them.

There comes a time when we have to lay down the past. Isaiah 43:18–19 declares, *Do not remember the former things, nor consider the things of old. Behold, I will do a new thing; now it shall spring forth; shall you not know it? I will even make a road in the wilderness and rivers in the desert.*

This scripture verse means you can expect God to do a new thing in your life every day of your life if you need Him to. He had to give Joseph a new beginning over and over again. And He will do the same thing for you, because He is no respecter of persons.

Joseph Stayed Connected to God

How did Joseph survive emotionally in a crazy, mixed-up world? How did he retain his sanity in circumstances that must have been extremely challenging and frustrating for him? The first thing he did was seek a close, personal relationship with God.

Many people know about God, but they don't let Him take an active role in their lives unless their back is up against the wall or they're struck by a gut-wrenching tragedy. But that's a foolish approach to take because God can help you avoid pitfalls in the first place. And He can also help you by preparing you ahead of time for trials by telling you things to come and showing you a way out.

So, I encourage you to stay close to the Lord every day. Don't wait until you find yourself in unbearable circumstances before you call on Him. Don't miss hearing the still, small voice of the Lord leading you on a daily basis.

Joseph had a close, personal relationship with God. No matter how many challenges he went through, he found grace to help him in time of need. And the reason he found God's grace and favor was because he was looking for them! Jesus said in Matthew 7:7, *Ask, and it will be given to you; seek, and you will find; knock, and it will be opened to you.*

Joseph was looking for God's grace, and the Lord was with him. He was serving God, loving Him, praising Him, listening to His voice, and searching for His will for his life. He was declaring, "I may be in jail, I may be a slave, but I love You, God, with all of my heart, my mind, and my strength."

Do you love God with everything that's within you? Or do you love Him only when things are going well for you? Joseph was sold out to God with his whole being, no matter how good or bad his circumstances were. And when opportunity came knocking, He was spiritually prepared to step up and enter into the deliverance God had for him.

Joseph Had a Powerful Sense of Purpose

The second thing Joseph did to survive emotionally during his trials was to develop and maintain a strong sense of purpose and destiny in his life. Remember, Joseph had two visions, two dreams, and his brothers hated him because of his life's vision and his sense of purpose.

Let's examine Joseph's first dream for a moment. He said, "Brothers, I saw you and me out working in the field, binding sheaves." I tell you, if God has put a vision in your heart, it is going to include work. James 2:17 declares that faith without works is dead. I thank God for faith, but I also thank God for the times when we get up out of our comfort zone and act on our faith.

Don't be satisfied with mediocrity. Strive for God's best. Give it your all. Joseph was an excellent worker. That's how he achieved such a high position in Potiphar's house. And I've got news. God is an excellent God, and He raised you up to be a person of excellence and a person of work.

Then Joseph had a second dream in which he saw the sun, moon, and eleven stars bow down to him, representing his father, mother, and brothers. This second vision showed Joseph his purpose, his mission in life—to be a great leader of his people.

Even while he was in prison, Joseph still had a vision for his future. He still had a calling from God. There was no way life could be over for him because his dream hadn't come to pass.

Perhaps God has placed a dream or a vision in your heart, but with all the commotion that's going on around you, you're wondering, *How can this ever come to pass? Is the box too tight? Are the walls too high? Is the time too short?* The answer is no. If the vision hasn't come to pass, it's not over for you yet.

Don't Get Bitter, and Don't Quit

The third thing Joseph did to survive emotionally in hard times was this: he refused to let people make him bitter; he let them make him better. Joseph did not allow the actions of others to determine his attitude. It's been said that your attitude in life determines your altitude. That's because if you allow bitterness or a negative attitude to pollute your mind, it's going to drag you down. But if you keep your attitude focused on the Lord, you're always going to rise to the top.

Joseph could have let anger and resentment toward his brothers get down into his spirit. He could have let a bad attitude creep in when Potiphar's wife lied about him and he was cast into prison. He could have given up hope of ever seeing his God-given dreams come to pass when the chief butler didn't tell Pharaoh about him. But Joseph just kept on doing his best in the situation he was in. He kept on seeking the Lord. He kept on trusting in God. He refused to stay bitter, and he refused to give up.

One day Pharaoh dreamed a dream that none of his wise men could interpret (Genesis 41). The chief butler suddenly remembered the young Jewish man who had interpreted his dream, so Pharaoh quickly had Joseph brought to him from prison.

That tells me that when one door shuts, you can expect God to open another door in your life. The new door may be different from the one you thought it would be. You've got to stop trying to figure everything out. Just trust God to open the right door at the right time.

God opened the door to Pharaoh's palace for Joseph, and he walked through it. He interpreted Pharaoh's dream, telling him that there would be seven years of abundance, which would be followed by seven years of famine in Egypt.

Then Joseph urged Pharaoh to appoint a wise administrator to gather up the crops during the seven years of plenty so there would be enough food stored up for the years of famine. Pharaoh was so pleased by Joseph's ability to interpret dreams, and also by his extraordinary wisdom, that he appointed him to be his right-hand man—his second in command!

When famine struck the land of Canaan where Joseph's brothers lived, they also ran out of food. So their father, Jacob, sent them to Egypt to buy provisions. Now, who do you suppose they had to ask for those provisions? Pharaoh's chief administrator—none other than Joseph, their long-lost brother (Genesis 42).

As his brothers bowed before him that day, no doubt Joseph remembered his dream about his brothers' sheaves bowing down to his sheaf. The dream wasn't being fulfilled in exactly the way he had pictured, but it was being fulfilled nonetheless.

Later, when Joseph revealed himself to his brothers, he could have yelled at them, "You dirty, rotten brothers! I'm the one you threw into the pit, the one you sold into slavery! You've got a lot of nerve coming to me for help!" He could have made them grovel in his presence. He could have returned evil for evil.

Instead, Joseph broke down and began to sob. He hadn't let his heart grow hard. He had kept his heart tender toward the Lord and toward his brothers. He threw his arms around them and exclaimed, "I'm Joseph! I'm the one you cast into the pit. I'm the one you sold into slavery. But don't be distressed or angry with yourselves for sending me here, because God sent me before you to preserve our lives by a great deliverance" (Genesis 45:1–7).

No matter what's happening to you right now, remember that God isn't lost and neither are you. You're not out in some vast, uncharted territory. God knows where you are and where you're going, because He has the road map of your life.

You may have ended up in a bad situation because of your own family as Joseph did. You may have had bad things happen in your childhood. But you don't have to live in the past. You don't have to let your attitude grow negative, or give up hope for your future. I tell you—you can let go of the awful situation that has tried to keep you down, and expect God to send you out on a brand-new journey in your life.

CHAPTER 14
HOW TO CLIMB OUT OF THE PIT

I feel in my spirit that some of you who are reading my words this very moment have the thought racing through your mind: *I've been under attack, and I've been standing against it; but I can't seem to break loose from this horrible situation.* Perhaps several months or even years have passed since you first found yourself falling into a pit of trouble, and it seems that no matter how hard you struggle to break free, you still haven't been able to climb up to freedom.

I remember a story in the Bible about a woman with a hemorrhage that had flowed from her body for twelve long years (Luke 8). I want you to see this woman with the eyes of your spirit. I want you to picture her slumped on the edge of her bed, weeping, feeling cut off from the world. She was desperate, bewildered, and at the end of her way.

Not only was the very life being drained out of her through this terrible flow of blood, but she also was ostracized and shunned by the people around her because of her condition. You see, in those days anyone who had an issue of blood was considered to be unclean.

You may be suffering from something that has cut you off from the rest of the world. Perhaps it's a crippling disease or paralysis, or maybe it's some type of pain that has wracked your body and kept you from living a normal, active life. If so, let this woman's testimony speak to you and build your faith for a miracle.

This woman was not only suffering in isolation, but the Bible also says that she suffered many things from many physicians—perhaps extensive medical tests and procedures. In fact, she had spent virtually all of her money searching for a cure, but her condition had only deteriorated.

Now, don't misunderstand what I'm saying here. This is not a slur against the medical profession. No doubt the doctors had genuinely tried to help her, but medicine was of such a primitive nature in those days that there was very little they could do for her. Even today, there are physical conditions that we currently have no medical cure for. And that can be a hard thing if you're the one who is sick and has no natural way to get better.

You may be at the same point this woman was. You may have endured many tests and treatments from many physicians. Although they've tried desperately to help you, the medical procedures were so grueling or had such horrible side effects that you've suffered almost more from the treatment than you've suffered from the disease. To top things off, instead of getting better, you've lost ground. Your condition has taken a nosedive, and now you're at your wit's end. That's exactly where this woman found herself. Then something happened that dramatically changed her life.

She heard about Jesus! The Amplified Bible says, *She had heard the reports concerning Jesus* (Mark 5:27). The Living Bible says, *She heard all about the wonderful miracles Jesus did.*

Most people alive today have heard at least something about Jesus. But did you know that you can go to church all of your life and hear about Jesus with your physical ears and still never hear about the real Jesus with your spiritual ears?

Somehow, it may not have registered in your spirit who Jesus really is. Perhaps you haven't grasped that His is the only power that can wash away your sins, heal every disease that's invaded your body, set you free from whatever circumstances you're in, and deliver you from whatever is troubling your soul.

When the woman with the hemorrhage of blood heard about Jesus, it dawned on her that it was the Lord's nature to heal. She immediately got excited about it and began to declare out loud, *If I can touch his clothing, I will be healed* (Matthew 9:21 NIV). The

Amplified Bible says that she kept repeating the words over and over again: *If I only touch His garment, I shall be restored to health.*

If you've ever faced a life-and-death battle of your faith, if you've ever taken your stand on God's Word and declared the Scriptures out loud day and night, then you understand what this woman was doing. She was fighting for her life with the words of her mouth. Proverbs 18:21 tells us, *Death and life are in the power of the tongue.*

When you're believing God for a healing and you're proclaiming the healing Scriptures by faith over your body, then you can expect those Scriptures to build up and strengthen your faith. As you continue to focus on who God is and what He has promised you in His Word, the truth that He's your healer will come alive deep in your soul, and nothing will be able to shake you from it—no heartbreaking reports from the doctor, no symptoms raging in your body, no negative words spoken over you.

The truth that He is your Provider, your Restorer, and your Helper will come alive in you. And you won't allow bad news, poor job forecasts, family problems, or anything else put a stop to what you're believing God to do for you. You will know that you know that you know that God's Word is true.

You may be thinking, "But I've been saying the Scriptures and saying the Scriptures, and I'm still in the same condition I was in before I started saying them." Just keep proclaiming God's Word in faith. He said in Isaiah 55:11, *My word...shall not return to Me void, but it shall accomplish what I please, and it shall prosper in the thing for which I sent it.* What did God send His Word to do? Psalm 107:20 declares that He sent His Word to heal you and deliver you from any destruction that would try to overtake your life.

God's Word will not return void. As long as you obey His Word, speak His Word, and do the things that He has spoken in your heart to do, you can expect His Word to accomplish what He sent it to do in your life.

You may say, "But I've suffered so long!" This woman had suffered for many years, but she still received her deliverance. God's Word accomplished what He sent it to do in her life.

Now, let me ask a very important question. What did this woman do to get her deliverance? She did what she felt the Holy Spirit was prompting her to do. And you also must do what you feel God speaking in your heart to do. It's so important to follow the leading of God's Spirit. When He directs us to do something, there's a reason for it. It's for our good. And by obeying Him, you just might be opening the door to your miracle.

This woman's miracle started when she began to say what God said about her situation, and she kept on speaking a word of healing over her life until she was healed. Saying the Word is such a powerful force for your deliverance. No matter how strongly you believe God's Word, it doesn't begin to move your mountain of problems out of your way until you speak it with your mouth in faith, and then believe what you said will come to pass.

Many people have rejected the teaching that you should confess your faith through the words you speak, but the very basis of the Christian faith is the confession of Jesus Christ as Lord and Savior. Romans 10:9–10 declares, *If you confess with your mouth the Lord Jesus and believe in your heart that God has raised Him from the dead, you will be saved. For with the heart one believes unto righteousness, and with the mouth confession is made unto salvation.* I tell you, it's absolutely vital for you to speak God's words continually, and then watch as His miracle-working power begins to blast mountains of obstacles out of your way.

Luke's Gospel gives us another important clue about why this woman received her healing from the Lord. Luke 8:47 (AMP) says, *She declared in the presence of all the people for what reason she had touched Him and how she had been instantly cured.*

You need to have a sense of purpose about you when you go to God. You can't simply think, "Well, I'll drift along and somehow, some way, God will do for me what I need done." It doesn't work that way. You must focus your faith on what you want from the Lord this very moment. I don't mean tomorrow; I mean today.

Press Through All the Obstacles

You may be thinking, "Richard, you don't know all the obstacles I'm facing. I've wrestled so hard to get a breakthrough, but I seem to be at a standstill." This woman faced more obstacles than most of us have ever faced, but she refused to back down on her faith.

Let's think about her situation for a moment. First of all, her condition had dragged on for twelve long years. She was probably skin and bones. A stream of blood was hemorrhaging from her body. No doubt she felt lightheaded, perhaps on the verge of passing out. Yet somehow she managed to get up that morning, get dressed, and go out and fight her way through the crowd that surrounded Jesus.

She wasn't even supposed to come in contact with other people. After all, the flow of blood meant that she was considered unclean. Besides, how could she possibly get through to Jesus? The Amplified Bible says that *a great crowd kept following Him, and pressed Him from all sides [so as almost to suffocate Him].*

I can imagine this woman crouching down and crawling through the mass of people surrounding Jesus, brushing them aside in a gentle but determined way. "Please excuse me, but I've got to get to the Master. You see, I've had this hemorrhage of blood for twelve years. I've spent all of my money trying to get well, but I'm growing weaker. Sir, please excuse me. Ma'am, won't you let me through?"

Suddenly she saw the Lord standing before her. She could see His sandals and His robe, and His prayer shawl wrapped around His body—the garment she had been straining with all of her might to touch. Jesus' prayer shawl was the same type of garment that was worn by the rabbis in that day, and its tassels represented the Word of God.

This woman was hungry for God's Word. She knew that her deliverance was in His promises. She had been speaking God's Word, confessing it with her mouth, and believing it in her heart. Now, as a point of contact to release her faith, she was ready to reach out and touch the Word of God.

When she grabbed the border of Jesus' garment, it was as if somebody flipped a switch and turned on the electricity. The power of God surged through her body, and the Bible says that Jesus whirled around and said, "Who touched Me?"

No doubt the disciples glared at Him in dismay. I can picture Peter blurting out, "Are you kidding me? Everybody is brushing up against You. Everybody is crying out, 'Jesus, touch me! Jesus, heal me!' And now You want to know who touched You? Believe me, we don't have any idea who touched You."

Now, think about all the commotion that was going on around the Master that day. This woman had to press through some major roadblocks to receive her deliverance. But when she saw all the people, she didn't throw up her hands and say, "Oh, the crowd is too big! There's no way I can get to Jesus." She didn't declare, "There's no way I can get a seat on the front row of that healing service, so I'm not going to go."

When trouble comes your way, you'd better do something about it. Get down on your knees, fall on your face before the Lord, jump to your feet, hop on your bicycle or put on your rollerblades, take a plane, take a train, take a taxi, have a friend bring you, do whatever you need to do, but get yourself into the presence of the Lord.

You may be able to meet with God right there in your own living room, or you may need to go to a healing crusade or watch a healing television program. I don't know what you need to do, but the Lord knows. Ask Him for His guidance, and then be quick to obey what He speaks in your heart.

Your Faith Has Made You Well

As soon as the woman touched the hem of Jesus' garment—her point of contact—it was time for her to start thanking God for her healing. It was time for her to rejoice in her soul because Jesus' word to her said that she was healed.

Think about what an experience this must have been for the woman. When she awakened that morning, she was terribly weak from the condition that had battered her body for so many years. She was probably beaten down in her spirit because she had been an outcast for so long. She'd been told there was no hope for her. Medical science had no other help to offer her. She was at the end of her rope when she touched Jesus' garment.

Then, all of a sudden, everything changed. When the Master asked who touched Him, she confessed what had happened in her body. She was bold in her faith, and Jesus rewarded her faith with an extraordinary miracle.

I want you to listen to what Jesus said to this woman next. He called her *Daughter.* And I know what a daughter means to her daddy, for I surely know what my daughters mean to me. In that one word, the love of Jesus flooded through every fiber of her being. *Daughter,* He called her. Then He said, *Your faith has made you well.*

Notice He did not say, "My overwhelming power has made you well," even though His power certainly was overwhelming. He didn't say, "My high-powered preaching has made you well." He didn't say, "The compassion of My Father has made you well." He didn't say, "Somebody else's faith has made you well."

He said, "Daughter, *your faith* has made you well."

If her faith made her whole, then your faith can make you whole too, because God is no respecter of persons. Romans 12:3 declares that God has given to every person the measure of faith they need for a miracle.

I believe you need to hear the Lord saying to you right now, "My son, My daughter." You need to hear it deep within your soul. You need to hear Him saying to you, "Your faith is healing your body. Your faith is blasting away the thing that has been troubling you, the thing you feel can't get any worse."

By your faith, you can cast that problem out. Just reach out and grab hold of the hem of Jesus' garment. Begin to call down your healing, your provision, your deliverance, or whatever answer to prayer that you're seeking from the Lord. If you stand on the Word of God when trouble comes, you can expect God to push Satan out of your way and turn your circumstances around for your good (Romans 8:28).

CHAPTER 15
YOU'RE COMING TO THE END OF AN UPHILL CLIMB

When you're running a race, the last stretch is always the most challenging. It's hard to describe the feeling that sweeps over you when you round that last turn and see the finish line in the distance before you. Many a great horse has seemingly run out of leg power by the time it entered the home stretch. But then something in the horse's spirit took over, and it began to run with heart.

When it seems as though all of hell's forces are arrayed against you, you may feel that you can't keep going. But that's when your heart takes over! However, if it hasn't dawned on you that you're coming to the end of an uphill climb—that your miracle is just ahead of you—then it's not easy for your heart to take over.

Probably one of the best illustrations I could give you of what I'm talking about is the story in Luke 5:17–26 of a man who had been down for a long time, paralyzed, his limbs completely lifeless. But he had four friends who cared enough to lift him up, and they took him to the top of an uphill climb.

Thank God for someone who will pick you up when you're knocked down, when you're strapped financially, when you're gripped by a spirit of aloneness, when it feels as if the props have been knocked out from under you.

That's what these four men did. They lifted up their friend who was paralyzed, struck down by a terrible, crippling paralysis, and they declared, "We're going to take you to Jesus!"

I can picture them hurrying through the busy streets of Capernaum, carrying their friend on a stretcher and telling him miracle stories about Jesus.

As they passed through the dusty streets, surely they must have said, "Did you hear about the man who was blind and Jesus Christ spat on the ground and made a mudpack out of the spittle, then smeared it on the man's eyes, and he was healed?" (See John 9.)

They may have said to him, "Did you hear about how the Lord raised Jairus' daughter from her deathbed?" (See Luke 8:41–56.) Or, "Did you hear about the way Jesus multiplied a few loaves and fishes and fed five thousand men?" (See Matthew 14:15–21.) I know if I had been carrying my friend to Jesus, I would have been filling him full of faith-building, miracle testimonies!

When the men arrived at the house where the Lord was preaching, there was such a crowd that they couldn't get through the door. There was seemingly no way for them to get to Jesus.

And that's where a lot of people are today. They have run head-on into a major obstacle, and they are just sitting there, staring at it, while the miracle they're believing for could be just beyond their fingertips.

There are plenty of people in the world today who will tell you that you cannot "get through the door." Everywhere you turn you'll see signs that read: *Do Not Enter.* Somebody will always be happy to inform you, "Yes, God can save you from your sins, but the days of miracles are over. God's supernatural power fizzled out with the last of the apostles."

May the Lord deliver us from that type of teaching, because the Jesus I know has miracles for us today!

The four men who took their friend to Jesus were rebuffed. All the doors were closed to them, but they refused to take no for an answer. Why? Because they believed they were coming to the end of an uphill climb. They believed their friend was about to be healed, once and for all.

What did they do? They hauled their friend, stretcher and all, onto the roof, and then they did something totally unorthodox. They tore the tiling off that roof one by one and then lowered the paralytic man down into the crowd right in front of Jesus. The four men literally began to raise the roof for their victory.

Grab Hold of Your Miracle

Can you imagine it? The room was jammed to the rafters. Jesus Christ was preaching and teaching the Word of God. All of a sudden the crowd gasped, their attention drawn toward the ceiling as a loud scratching noise came from the roof.

A trickle of dust began to sift down onto their hair and faces. All at once, a sparkle of sunlight flashed through the hole in the roof. Then the hole started to widen, and Jesus glanced up just as the men began to lower their friend down into the room on a pallet.

I want you to notice what the Bible says next: *Jesus saw their faith.* Whose faith did He see? The faith of the man's four friends! When He saw their faith, He fastened His eyes on the paralyzed man and declared, "Your sins are forgiven."

Now, don't you think that was an unusual thing for the Lord to say? The man was paralyzed, his whole body limp and lifeless. He could not take one single step alone. Clearly he needed a miracle of healing, and yet Jesus proclaimed, "Man, your sins are forgiven."

The Lord cut right through to the heart of the matter because He recognized that the man wasn't right with God. And the man also knew he wasn't right with God. When you and I get into the holy presence of the Lord, we can feel His Holy Spirit microscope examining us, and we know whether or not we need to get something straightened out with Him.

Jesus recognized that the man was in need of restoration and forgiveness. So He told the man, "Your sins are forgiven." In a flash, the man's heart was transformed. His sins were washed away. His whole life was made brand new.

That episode caused quite an uproar among the religious leaders. Only God Himself could forgive sins, they reasoned.

But the Bible says that the Lord perceived their thoughts. So He asked them, *"Why are you reasoning in your hearts? Which is easier, to say, 'Your sins are forgiven you,' or to say, 'Rise up and walk'? But that you may know that the Son of Man has power on earth to forgive sins"—He said to the man who was paralyzed, "I say to you, arise, take up your bed, and go to your house"* (Luke 5:22–24).

There is always a special moment in your life and mine—a moment when we must put our faith in gear and act on the words of Jesus. The paralyzed man came to that special moment. He had to make a choice to act.

His friends had struggled to carry him to the top of an uphill climb. They had knocked down every obstacle and raised the roof for victory. They had lowered the man down into the presence of Jesus. The Lord had forgiven his sins, and then He cut through all the fat when He said, "Take up your bed and walk!" It was a special moment. It was up to the man to act.

There always comes a time when it's your turn to act. What are you going to do when Jesus speaks to you? Are you going to obey Him? Or are you going to argue, "Well, now, let me think about it for a moment"? I tell you, you've got to grab hold of your miracle the way a drowning man grabs for his last breath of air.

When Jesus gave the word to the paralyzed man, "Arise, take up your bed and walk," everybody was astonished, and they watched to see what would happen next.

The ball was in the paralyzed man's court. He must have said to himself, "Why shouldn't I go ahead and get up? I know I've been down for a long time, but I'm sick and tired of lying here on this bed of affliction. I want to go home. I want to give my wife a great big hug. I want to run and play ball with my children for the first time in years."

As soon as he decided to act on God's Word, the miracle power of the Lord hit him like a bolt of lightning. When the power of the Lord hits you and you respond to His power, a miracle can be transferred into your life.

Suddenly, the man's lifeless limbs surged with strength. He leaped to his feet, folded up his bed, and began to walk, completely healed by the power of God. Pandemonium broke loose in that house that day. There was an explosion of joy and a great celebration. Glory be to God, the paralyzed man made it to the end of an uphill climb.

God Never Takes You on a Downhill Slide

It's so important for you to reach out with your spirit and grab hold of the fact that you're coming to the end of an uphill climb. Aren't you glad that you're not caught on a downhill slide?

God never takes you on a downhill slide. He always takes you on an uphill climb. I believe it is His desire to lead every Christian to higher heights in life. But you must do your part and act on God's Word like the paralyzed man did when his four friends took him to Jesus.

Why should you settle for living in a horrible pit the rest of your life? If you're going through trouble, whatever you do, don't stop. Keep moving forward in your faith. Don't quit until you receive the miracle you need from the Lord.

CHAPTER 16
AVOIDING PITFALLS THE SECOND TIME AROUND

Why is it that some people seem to get yanked back down into the same old traps over and over again? They seem to be caught on a loop, and they can't get off. Of course, I don't believe anyone leaps out of bed in the morning and exclaims, "I believe I'll make a mistake today." That's not how it happens.

People don't purpose in their hearts to make a mistake, but we've all made enough mistakes in our lifetimes to sink a battleship! The big question is, are we learning from our mistakes? Do we avoid the pitfalls the second time around, or do we simply stumble headlong into the same old snares again and again?

The Bible teaches us clearly that if we'll repent and learn from our mistakes, our future can be radically changed. That means we've got to break free from the old patterns and avoid the same pitfalls the second time around.

Whatever You Do, Don't Run from God

The prophet Jonah was a man who made a huge mistake in his life, but when he learned from his mistake, the people in an entire city repented and gave their hearts to the Lord.

If you recall the background of Jonah's story, there was a large and wealthy city called Nineveh, but it was also a very wicked city. The Bible says that God began to search for a man to preach repentance to the thousands of citizens there.

The Lord found such a man in Jonah, and He spoke to him, saying, *Get up and go to the great city of Nineveh. Announce my judgment against it because I have seen how wicked its people are* (Jonah 1:2 NLT). In other words, "Tell them they are heading toward destruction and hell if they don't get their lives turned around."

This wasn't a happy message. But the Lord told Jonah to preach it anyway. Jonah knew exactly what God wanted him to do.

But Jonah made a big mistake. Instead of heading straight for Nineveh, he traveled to the seacoast town of Joppa, where he booked passage on a boat sailing across the Mediterranean Sea to Tarshish, 180 degrees in the opposite direction from Nineveh. Really, that ship was taking Jonah away from the Lord.

There are many vehicles in this world that are taking people away from God today—drugs, apathy, greed, and so on. No matter who or what is leading you off the path that God has for you, you'd better get off the vehicle that's taking you away from God.

Why Did Jonah Run?

As I've studied this story from the Bible over the years, I've often asked myself, "Why did Jonah run from the Lord? Why do men and women try to run from the call of God on their lives?"

First of all, I believe Jonah ran because he was struggling with prejudice. You see, Jonah was Jewish, and Nineveh was a city filled with Gentiles. Jonah didn't want to go to Nineveh because the people were different from him.

The world today is steeped in prejudice. People turn their backs on others because of the color of their skin, their ethnic background, and even the way they talk. The bottom line was that Jonah did not want to preach the Gospel to a city of Gentiles. There are many people today who have a similar prejudice in their hearts, and they're not doing what God has called them to do because they don't want to be aligned with a particular group of people.

Every time I preach in one of the great African-American churches around the world, it would be easy for someone to say, "What is that white guy doing up there ministering?" The answer is simple. I go where God tells me to go. And God is bigger than ethnic backgrounds, skin color, or any of the human things that we use to create a sense of "us" versus "them." He wants all people to be saved, regardless of what particular group they do or don't belong to.

I believe the second reason Jonah ran was that he was more concerned about his reputation than he was about the Word of God. He was terrified of what someone might think of him if he went to Nineveh. He didn't want to risk embarrassment by standing on the street corners of that wicked city and shouting, "Forty days from now, Nineveh will be destroyed! If you don't repent, God is going to wipe you off the face of the earth!"

Jonah didn't want to appear foolish, but the apostle Paul declared in 1 Corinthians 4:10, "I am a fool for Christ!" He said, *I am not ashamed of the gospel of Christ, for it is the power of God to salvation for everyone who believes* (Romans 1:16). And I, too, am not ashamed to be called a fool for Christ. In fact, 1 Corinthians 1:27 tells us that God takes the things that the world calls foolish and uses them to confound the wise!

I believe the third reason Jonah ran from God's calling is that he thought the Lord would draft somebody else to do the job. A lot of people today have the mistaken idea that if they'll just hide from the limelight a little bit longer, God will get somebody else to do what He has called them to do.

But I've got news for you. It's no accident that you're alive in this hour. You were born for such a time as this. God wants you to do what He's called you to do. He's not looking for someone else to do it. Besides, there's no place where you can hide from the call of God upon your life.

That brings me to the fourth reason why I believe Jonah tried to run from the Lord. He actually thought that he could run away from the Almighty. But where can you go that God isn't there? What corner of the earth can you travel to where God isn't present? It's impossible to run away from God's presence (Psalm 139:7–10).

Jonah thought he could run away from the Lord. But he didn't reckon with the One whose hands scooped out the beds for the oceans, flung the stars from His fingertips, and hung this world on nothing. He didn't reckon with the mighty hand of God.

As soon as the ship got under way, Jonah went down into the bottom of the boat, curled up with his pillow, and fell asleep. In a moment's time, a violent storm erupted. The boat popped and cracked in the wind as the sails started to rip from their masts. The tempest was so fierce that the ship lurched and rocked dangerously atop the crashing waves.

The sailors were wild with fear, and they began to cry out to their gods for help. Finally, the captain went below and awakened Jonah, demanding, "How can you sleep at a time like this? Get up and pray to your God, and see if He'll have mercy and save us!"

In sheer desperation, the crew decided to cast lots to find out who was causing the storm. When the lot fell on Jonah, he admitted, "I'm running away from the Lord. Throw me overboard, and the sea will become calm. This storm is because of me."

Those men didn't have to hear Jonah's words a second time. They picked him up and hurled him into the sea, and the storm stopped.

The Bible says that God had prepared "a great fish" especially for Jonah, and it gulped him down whole. The fish had a body that not only accommodated the entire length of Jonah's body but also kept him alive for three days and three nights. Now, that's some fish!

If you're running from God, I want you to know that God has a special place prepared for you to get back into a right relationship with Him. It may be through the help of family and friends. It may be through your church. It may be just you and God in prayer. But God has a special place prepared just for you to come back to His will for your life. When you get into that place, you're going to learn from your mistakes, and God is going to show you how to avoid the pitfalls the second time around.

When Jonah Obeyed God, a Whole City Was Born Again

Jonah found himself trapped inside the belly of that great fish, and he began to cry out to the Lord in his anguish and despair. I can just imagine him wading through the deepest, darkest recesses of that fish's belly, calling upon God's mercy and crying out to the Lord, "If You'll only get me out of this mess, I'll obey You. Heavenly Father, I promise I'll learn from this mistake."

That's what God is looking for. He's looking for someone who will walk in obedience to Him.

The instant Jonah declared, "God, I'll do whatever You tell me to do," that fish turned around, swam straight toward the shoreline, and vomited Jonah up on the sandy shores. When his feet touched the dry ground, Jonah didn't board another ship headed for Tarshish. No, he set out for Nineveh. He marched straight into the middle of town to obey God and preach the message the Lord gave him.

What a sight Jonah must have been as he began to shout, "Nineveh, you've got forty days to repent. That's all the time God is going to give you. If you don't repent, God is going to wipe you off the face of the earth." Jonah stood there in the boiling sun and preached his heart out.

The people were so jolted by Jonah's message that they believed him, fell down on their knees, and repented before the Lord. Even the king himself repented in sackcloth and ashes.

Nineveh had been heading straight toward destruction, but when Jonah obeyed the Lord, much to his shock and amazement, God allowed the citizens of that city to live. In the Lord's great mercy, love, and grace, thousands of people whose lives were hanging in the balance received salvation.

God Forgives Your Mistakes and Forgets Them

I've stumbled and made many mistakes in my lifetime. I remember one time when I was very young, my father asked me, "Richard, you've made a mistake, haven't you?"

"Yes, I have," I replied.

Then he reassured me, "If you'll give your mistake to God, if you'll repent and tell Him that you're sorry for it with all of your heart, I'll stand with you 100 percent."

I realized what he said was absolutely true. And it was just that simple. So I prayed with him, and I repented to God and received His forgiveness. Wow! That was an amazing experience, and although that was many, many years ago, I still remember it like it was yesterday.

And that's wonderful advice to you today! So many times, our mistakes dog our tracks day and night. They hang over us like a cloud, haunting our every waking moment. But thank God, we serve a God we can run to when we slip up and make a mistake. Psalm 40:2 tells us that the God we serve can handle the miry clay of sin. He can lift us out of the deepest pit, set our feet upon the Rock of salvation, and establish us.

Perhaps you've been running from the Lord like Jonah was. Or maybe you've been burdened down by a past mistake or sin. Whatever mistakes you may have made, when you repent, God removes your sins from you *as far as the east is from the west* (Psalm 103:12). In Hebrews 8:12 (KJV), God says, *I will be merciful... and their sins and their iniquities will I remember no more.* By the mighty power of the Lord, you can become a new person—a forgiven person.

Don't carry that old baggage of guilt and shame any longer. Cast your mistakes and burdens over onto the Lord, and open up your heart to Him as you pray this prayer out loud:

God, I give You my mistakes and my failures, and I turn my back on the past. I repent, and I look to Jesus as the Savior of my soul. I make a new confession that Jesus Christ is my Lord and Savior, my Healer, and the Forgiver of my sins. I commit my life to Him, and I won't get off the right road again. I'm a Jesus person, and I am forgiven! Amen.

And now, I can feel the fire of God's Spirit moving in me to pray:

Heavenly Father, I come to You in the mighty Name of the Savior, in the Name of the healing, delivering Christ, and I rebuke the satanic powers that are coming against my brother, my sister in the Lord. I speak to the situation and circumstances that are trying to wreck their dreams, and I rebuke their power. Satan, I command you in the Name of Jesus to stop tormenting my fellow brothers and sisters in the Lord! Release them now!

O God, I speak to every sea of disturbance, and I command it to be hushed to sleep.

I pray that the joy of the Lord will flood their hearts and drive away all the gloom. Lord, I call upon You now for Your mighty healing, delivering power to fill their lives and set them free.

My dear friend, I call upon a host of angels to cover you and protect you. I pray that God's loving, healing arms will surround you and that you'll feel His awesome power sweeping over your life.

In the Name of Jesus, I call forth the restoration of your hope for the future. I call forth the miracles your heart desires. May Jesus Christ of Nazareth lead you to safety and victory, and may He set you free from the hellish situations of life! Amen.

About the Author

Richard Roberts, D. Min., is Chief Executive Officer of the Oral Roberts Ministries. For over 30 years, he has conducted healing services throughout America and around the world. As a young boy, Richard often stood by his dad's side in the healing lines of Oral's tent cathedral, helping to pray for those who were sick. Today, his own international healing crusades are marked by a tremendous move of the Spirit, with people often reporting a broad range of healing miracles.

In addition, Richard heads the School of Miracles, a practical, biblically-based series of online courses designed to help Christians grow in their knowledge of God, their faith, and how to share God's miracle-working power with those in need. To date, more than 18,000 students in over 75 countries have participated.

Richard and his wife, Lindsay, co-host a daily television program, *The Place for Miracles.* He has authored a number of books, including *He's A Healing Jesus.* He also produces CDs, DVDs, and other faith-inspiring materials.

Richard Roberts
P.O. Box 2187
Tulsa, OK 74102-2187

www.oralroberts.com

For prayer anytime, call **The Abundant Life Prayer Group** at **918-495-7777**, or contact us on the web at **www.oralroberts.com/prayer**.